A. FRANK SMITH, JR. LIBRARY CENTER
Southwestern University
Georgetown, Texas 78626

W9-BAV-685

WITHDRAWN

Prove me . . . .
if I will not open you
the windows of heaven.
                    Malachi

PRESENTED TO
CODY MEMORIAL LIBRARY
BY
KELLOGG FOUNDATION

THE LORD IS MY SHEPHERD

THE LORD
IS
MY SHEPHERD

STORIES FROM THE BIBLE
PICTURED IN BIBLE LANDS

ARRANGED AND ILLUSTRATED

By

NANCY BARNHART

74878

NEW YORK
CHARLES SCRIBNER'S SONS

CODY MEMORIAL LIBRARY
SOUTHWESTERN UNIVERSITY
GEORGETOWN, TEXAS

COPYRIGHT 1949 BY
NANCY BARNHART

PRINTED IN THE UNITED STATES OF AMERICA
F-9.62 [MH]
ALL RIGHTS RESERVED. NO PART OF THIS BOOK
MAY BE REPRODUCED IN ANY FORM WITHOUT
THE PERMISSION OF CHARLES SCRIBNER'S SONS

C
220.9
B266l

FOREWORD

The stories in this book are intended as an introduction to the Bible, an invitation to enter and discover the wonders of the Book of Books. Trying to compete with the majestic words of the King James Version would be pure folly. But to point the way to that version by awakening interest in the Bible may not be too ambitious.

After you read the stories, you may turn to the King James Version and find in full detail every passage used here in a briefer form. At the back of our book is a list which gives the original passages for every story.

When I travelled through Bible lands a few years ago, I was delighted to find people in those countries actually reaping, threshing, baking, building walls, and wearing simple square-cut garments as did their ancestors in the days of the Book. To Western eyes it may appear strange for clothes and customs to follow the same pattern for thousands of years; yet in the East it seems most logical to esteem what has proved useful to one's father and grandfather and great-grandfather. The farmer boys reaping in the fields might well be Joseph and his brothers, singing to the rhythm of their flashing sickles. There is an art in these movements, learned through generations, as there is an art in the tilt of the water jar balanced on the modern Rebecca's head.

Many of the houses shown in our pictures were erected on the site of fallen buildings simply by putting the stones together again, with some new ones from the hills, and some borrowed from neighboring ruins, a ready source of material.

And so the wall of Jerusalem, golden with the color of limestone weathered by long exposure to sunlight, embodies a great history of ups and downs. The topmost stories are the work of Suleiman the Magnificent, after the Arab conquest in the Middle ages, with some English restorations of recent years. Underneath are the remains of solid Roman masonry. And so down below the present level of earth to the time of Nehemiah and older men who built and rebuilt aad repaired. Portions of David's wall have been unearthed.

The rough stone dwelling in Bethlehem pictured on page 107 might have been erected in any age, as also the quaint houses sketched in Hebron or in Nain, which belong to no special period of architecture. For old houses in Palestine today often resemble the picture-book carvings on bas-reliefs of ancient Assyria, buildings that have taken shape around the barest needs of shelter and convenience.

In sketching the works of nature, it is a satisfaction to know that these are the eternal hills of Judea. This is the River Jordan flowing today as it did when Naaman dipped into its water and was healed of leprosy. Just such bright sunshine as this we see today, sparkled on the waves and outlined the far shores when the Master looked from Capernaum across Lake Galilee.

NANCY BARNHART

CONTENTS

ILLUSTRATIONS

THE OLD TESTAMENT

IN THE BEGINNING

IN the beginning God created the heaven and the earth.

And the earth was waste and void; and darkness covered the abyss. And the spirit of God brooded over the face of the deep.

And God said, "Let there be light!" And there was light. God saw that the light was good; and God divided the light from the darkness. He called the light Day, and the darkness He called Night. And there was evening and morning, the first day.

And God said, "Let there be a firmanent in the midst of the waters, to divide them in two." God made the firmament, and divided the waters which were under the firmament from the waters which were above the firmament. And it was so. And God called the firmament Heaven. Evening came and morning came, the second day.

And God said, "Let the waters under the heaven be gathered together, and let the dry land appear." And it was so. And God called the dry land Earth, and the waters He called Seas; and God saw that it was good.

And God said, "Let the earth bring forth grass, and plants that have seed, each of its own kind, and fruit-trees that have fruit with seed of every kind." And it was so; the earth had grass and plants with their seed, and trees with fruit of every kind. And God saw that it was good. And evening came and morning came, the third day.

And God said, "Let there be lights in heaven, to give light on the earth, and to mark the days and seasons and years." And it was so. God made two great lights, the greater to rule the day and the lesser to rule the night. Then He made the stars. And He saw that it was very good. And evening came and morning came, the fourth day.

And God said, "Let the water have life moving in it, and let birds fly in the open space of heaven." So God created great whales, and all the living things of the sea, and all the winged fowls of heaven. And God blessed them, saying, "Grow and increase; fill the sea and the air." And evening came and morning came, the fifth day.

And God said, "Let the earth have living creatures of every kind, cattle and wild beasts and all things that creep along the ground." So God made the cattle and wild beasts and creeping things of every kind. And God saw that it was good. And evening came and morning came, the sixth day.

And God said, "Let us make man as Our own image, Our own likeness; and let them have dominion over the fish of the sea and over the birds of the air, and over the animals, and over every creeping thing that creeps along the ground."

So God created man as His own image, His own likeness. Male and female he created them. And God blessed them, and said to them, "Grow and increase; fill the world, and have dominion over the fish of the sea and the birds of the air, and over the animals and over every thing that creeps along the ground."

And God said, "See, I have given you every plant that has seed on the face of the earth, and every fruit-bearing tree with its seed; they shall be food for you. And for every animal and every bird and every creeping thing I have given the green plants for food." And it was so.

And God looked at everything that He had made, and He saw that it was very good.

Thus the heavens and the earth were finished, with all their hosts. And on the seventh day God's work was finished, and He rested on that day from all His work. And God blessed the seventh day and called it a holy day.

Now the Lord God made man out of the dust of the ground, and breathed life into his nostrils, and man became a living soul.

And the Lord God planted a garden in the east, and there He put the man whom He had made. And out of the ground the Lord God made every tree that is beautiful and good for food, the tree of life also in the middle of the garden, and the tree of knowledge of good and evil.

And the Lord God took the man and put him into the garden, to keep it and care for it, saying to him "You may eat the fruit of every tree in the garden, except the tree of knowledge of good and evil. You shall not eat of it, for if you eat of this tree, you shall die."

And from the ground the Lord God made every animal and every bird, and brought them to Adam to see what he would call them. And Adam gave a name to every animal on earth and every bird of the air.

And the Lord God said, "It is not good that the man should be alone. I will make a helper for him." So the Lord God put Adam into a deep sleep, and He took one of his ribs. From the rib He made a woman, and brought her to the man. Adam called her Eve because she was the mother of all living.

Now the serpent was more crafty than any other beast of the field. And the serpent said to the woman, "Has God said you shall not eat the fruit of every tree in the garden?"

"We may eat the fruit of all the trees in the garden," said the woman, "except the tree that grows in the middle of the garden. If we eat of it, or touch it, we must die."

The serpent said, "Surely you will not die. If you eat the fruit, it will make you wise."

Now since it was good to look at and sweet to taste, and would make her wise, she took the fruit and gave some to her husband.

A garden in the East; sketched in Egypt

When they had eaten it, they were ashamed, and hid from the Lord.

And they heard the voice of the Lord God walking in the garden in the cool of the day.

And the Lord God called to Adam, "Where are you? Have you eaten the fruit of the tree?"

Adam said, "The woman You gave me, she offered me the fruit, and I ate it."

"What is this you have done?" said the Lord God to Eve. And Eve said, "The serpent tempted me, and I ate the fruit."

Then the Lord God said to the serpent, "On your belly shall you crawl and dust shall you eat all the days of your life. To the woman he said, "You shall have sorrow and children born in sorrow." And to Adam he said, "Toil shall be yours, thorns and trouble, till you turn to dust again." So He drove them out from the garden, and set angels to the eastward and a flaming sword, which turned every way to guard the tree of life.

NOAH AND THE ARK

ADAM had many children, who spread far and wide over the earth. And when there were many people in the world, they became very wicked.

Then God was sorry that He had made man on the earth, and he said, "I will destroy man whom I have created, both man and beast and the creeping things and the birds of the air."

But He thought of Noah, who was honest and good; and He said to Noah, "Build yourself an ark of gopher wood with rooms in it and cover it with pitch. For I shall send a flood over the earth, and everything that is on the earth shall die.

"In this ark you will be safe, you and your sons, and your wife, and your sons' wives. Take with you into the ark two of every living creature, birds and beasts and all things that walk on the earth. And take food for all."

So Noah built the ark, as God had said, and went into it with his wife and his sons, Shem and Ham and Japheth, and his sons' wives. And the animals went in two by two, male and female.

And rain fell on the earth forty days and forty nights, for the fountains of sky and sea were broken open; and the highest mountains were covered by the flood. But when the waters came to where the ark was they lifted it up, so that it floated above the earth. Thus Noah and his family and all that were in the ark were kept alive, while water covered the earth.

And after a hundred and fifty days God remembered Noah and every living thing that was with him in the ark, and God sent a wind to pass over the earth. Then the rain from heaven stopped, and the waters grew less.

Now the ark came to rest on Mount Ararat. Noah opened the window and sent out a raven; but the raven flew away over the water.

Then Noah sent out a dove. When the dove found no place to rest the sole of her foot, she returned to the ark. So he put out his hand and took her into the ark with him.

After seven days he sent her again, and she came in the evening with an olive leaf in her beak; so Noah knew that the flood had gone down.

He waited seven days, and again he sent her out. And this time she did not return.

Now Noah removed the covering of the ark, and he saw that the earth was dry.

And God said to Noah, "Come out of the ark, you and your wife and your sons and your sons' wives. Bring all the living creatures, for they are to increase and fill the world."

God blessed Noah and his sons, and said to them, "If you keep My laws no flood shall ever again destroy the earth. This will be a sign of My promise to you and to all living creatures forever; I shall set My rainbow in the clouds, and when I bring a cloud over the earth My rainbow shall be seen in it."

Noah welcomes the dove

FAITHFUL ABRAHAM

ABRAM lived in Ur of the Chaldees, where his father worshipped false gods. And the Lord said to Abram, "Leave your country, and your father's house, for a land that I will show you."

So Abram left his home and came to Canaan. And the Lord said, "Lift up your eyes, and look from where you are standing, to the north, the south, the east, and the west. For all the land which you see, I give to you and to your children for ever. Come, walk through the length and breadth of it; I give it to you."

Now Abram pitched his tent in Canaan, and built an altar to the Lord. And the Lord said to him, "Have no fear, Abram, for I am your shield and your exceedingly great reward."

Abram said, "Lord God, what can You give me, seeing that I have no children?"

Then God led Abram out under the sky and said, "Can you count the stars in heaven? As many as the

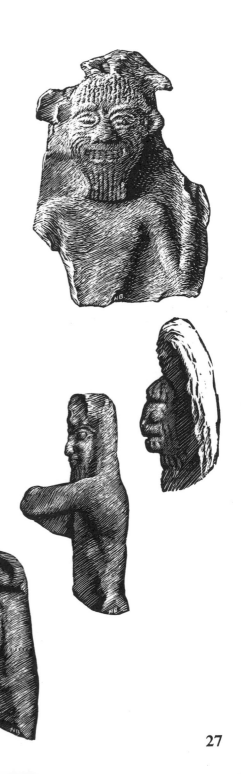

Chaldean images

stars in heaven shall be your children and your children's children."

Abram believed the Lord; in this he showed his true faith. And when Abram was ninety-nine years old the Lord said to him, "I am the Almighty God; walk before Me and be perfect. Your name shall be changed to Abraham; for I have made you a father of many nations."

And one day as Abraham was sitting at the door of his tent, God came to him and said, "Sarah your wife shall have a son."

But Sarah heard it, inside the tent, and laughed to herself. "Shall I have a son?" said she, "when I am old, and my husband also is old?"

The Lord said to Abraham, "Why did Sarah laugh? Is anything too hard for the Lord? When the time comes next year, Sarah will have a son."

And so it came about; when Abraham was a hundred years old, Sarah gave him a son. They called him "Isaac," meaning "Laughter," for Sarah said,

View from Bethel

Abraham sees the Promised Land

"God has made me laugh, and every one who hears of it will laugh with me."

When Isaac was old enough to be married, Abraham said to his trusted servant, "Go to my country, to my people, and find a wife for my son Isaac. The angel of the Lord will lead you to find him a wife from among my own kinsfolk."

So the servant took ten camels and went to Meso-

74878

Cody Memorial Library
Southwestern University
Georgetown, Texas

potamia, to the city of Abraham's brother Nahor.

It was evening when he arrived, and the women were coming to the well for water. He stood by the well with his camels, and prayed, "Lord, send me the chosen bride."

Just then a beautiful girl came from the well. He ran to meet her, and said, "Will you give me some water to drink?" She tipped her water jar, resting it on her hand, to let him drink. After this she drew water for the camels.

Then the servant took out a golden earring and two bracelets of gold, and gave them to her, and said, "Whose daughter are you?"

She told him that she was Rebekah, the daughter of Abraham's nephew, Bethuel.

"Praise be to the Lord God of my master Abraham!" said he, "for He has led me to my master's people."

Now Rebekah ran and told all this to her family,

and showed them the precious jewels.

And now her brother Laban came to where the man stood by the well, and said to him, "Come in, you who have been blessed by the Lord. Our house is ready for you, and there is room for your camels."

And the servant told his story, how he had come to find a wife for Abraham's son in Mesopotamia, and how God had answered his prayer.

Laban and Bethuel said, "It is the work of God."

Now the servant brought out jewels of silver and gold, and clothing for Rebekah and her brother and her mother.

So he ate and drank and rested that night. And in the morning Rebekah's family said to her, "Will you go with this man?"

She said, "I will go."

Then they gave her their blessing. And Rebekah and her maids mounted the camels and followed the servant into Canaan, to Abraham's house.

JACOB AND ESAU

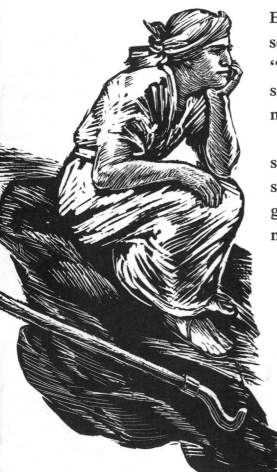

ISAAC and Rebekah had twin sons named Jacob and Esau. Esau, the first-born, was his father's delight because he was a hunter, rough and hairy; while the mother loved Jacob, who was a quiet man and lived in tents.

Jacob was cooking some lentil soup one day when Esau came in faint and hungry. "Give me some soup, I beg of you," he said. "I will," said Jacob, "if you will sell me your right to be called the eldest son." So Esau agreed, and sold his birthright for a mess of lentils.

Now when Isaac was old and his eyes were dim so that he could not see, he called Esau to him and said, "My son, take your quiver and your bow and go out to the field and get me some venison to make me the savory meat that I love. Bring it to me so

34

that I may eat, and that I may give you my blessing before I die."

Esau went out to the field to hunt for venison, and while he was gone, Rebekah prepared the dish for Isaac, with young goats' meat instead of venison; and she said to Jacob, "Take this to your father, and he will give you his blessing."

But Jacob said, "Esau my brother is a hairy man and I am not. My father may feel me and I shall seem to be a deceiver and he will not bless me."

"Obey me, my son," said Rebekah, and she put Esau's best clothes on Jacob and covered his hands and neck with the goats' skins.

So Jacob brought in the meat to Isaac, and said, "Father, this is your first-born, Esau, with the venison. Now give me your blessing."

But Isaac said, "How did you find it so quickly, my son?"

"Because the Lord sent it," said Jacob.

Then Isaac felt his son, and he said, "The voice is Jacob's, — but the hands are the hands of Esau. Are you truly my son Esau?"

And he said, "I am."

"Bring me the meat," said Isaac, "and kiss me, my son." And he gave him his blessing.

And it happened, as soon as Isaac had finished blessing Jacob, that Esau came in from the hunt.

When Esau found that Jacob had taken away his blessing, he vowed he would kill him.

The mother warned Jacob, "Your brother will kill you if you stay here. Go at once to Laban my brother in Padan-aram and stay until Esau forgets his rage." So Jacob went away towards his uncle's house.

At sunset he lay down to sleep, with stones of the field for his pillow. And he dreamed he saw a ladder from earth to heaven, with angels of God going up and down on it. And the Lord stood above it and said to Jacob, "I am the God of Abraham and of Isaac. I will give the land where you are lying to you and your children; they shall be a blessing to all nations on earth."

Jacob awoke and said, "Surely the Lord is in this place and I did not know it! This is the house of God, this is the gate of heaven. And he took the stone that he had put for his pillow and set it up as a pillar, and poured oil on it. And he called the place Bethel, (House of God); and he said, "If the Lord will bring me to my father's house again in peace, then He shall be my God."

And Jacob came to Padan-aram, and lived there twenty years and married Laban's two daughters and grew rich.

A ruined tower in Bethel

Then one day the Lord said to him, "Return now to your own country. I will be with you."

So Jacob set out for Canaan with his wives and children and servants and cattle, and sent messengers ahead to tell Esau he was coming.

The messengers returned to Jacob and said, "Your brother Esau is on the way to meet you, and with him are four hundred men."

Then Jacob prayed, "O Lord, I am not worthy of the least of Your mercies, but save me from my brother!"

And when he had crossed the brook Jabbok with his wives, Leah the tender-eyed and Rachel the beautiful, and all the rest of his family, he stayed alone that night beside the brook.

And there came a man, or angel, and wrestled with him till daybreak. And when the angel saw that he could not conquer Jacob, he touched his thigh and put it out of joint as he wrestled. And he said to Jacob, "Let me go, for the day is breaking!"

The Brook Jabbok

"I will not let you go until you bless me," said Jacob. Then the angel said, "From this time on, your name shall be no longer Jacob, but Israel, Prince of God."

And Jacob asked, "What is your name?"

"Why do you ask?" said the angel, and he blessed him there. Then Jacob said, "I have seen God face to face, and my life is saved."

Now he looked and saw his brother coming, and four hundred men with him. Jacob went ahead of his wives and children, bowing to the ground in front of Esau.

Esau ran to meet him, and embraced him and kissed him. And they wept.

"I have seen your face as though it were the face of God," said Jacob, "and you were pleased with me."

Thus Jacob came again to live in his own land. And the twelve sons of Jacob became the twelve tribes of Israel.

JOSEPH
AND HIS BROTHERS

AMONG the twelve sons of Israel there was one he loved best of all, named Joseph. And he gave him a coat of many colors.

The other sons hated Joseph because he was his father's favorite, and always dreaming dreams. Once he told them he had dreamed they were harvesting in the field, and all their sheaves of wheat came and bowed down to his sheaf.

His brothers said, "Shall you indeed be ruler over us?" And they hated him still more.

One day as they were pasturing their father's sheep, they saw Joseph coming across the field. "Here comes the dreamer," they said to one another. "Let us kill him, and see what becomes of his dreams!"

They took off his coat of many colors and threw him into a pit. But one of them happened to see an Ishmaelite caravan passing by on the way to Egypt; and he said, "Let us sell him to the Ishmaelites!"

So they lifted Joseph up out of the pit and sold him to the Ishmaelites, who took him into Egypt.

Then the brothers killed a young goat; and they dipped Joseph's coat in the blood and took it to their father. "See what we have found," they said, "Is this Joseph's coat?"

"It is my son's coat! Some wild beast has torn him to pieces!" cried the father. And he wept and mourned for his son, and refused to be comforted.

Now Joseph was in Egypt, where he had been sold to Potiphar, an officer of Pharaoh's, and captain of the guard.

And the Lord was with Joseph, and his master saw that the Lord gave success to everything that

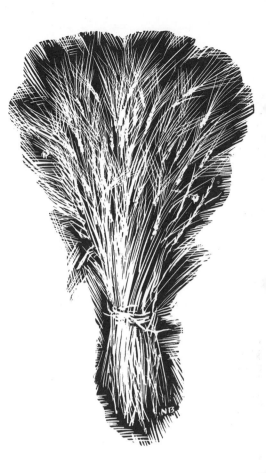

was put into Joseph's hand. So Potiphar gave him full charge over his household and all his possessions.

But Potiphar's wife told lies about Joseph and had him thrown into prison.

Still the Lord was with him; for the jail-keeper put all the prisoners under his care.

Into prison came the king's butler and baker who had in some way offended their master. One night both these men had curious dreams. And Joseph said to them, "Does not the interpreting of dreams belong to God? Tell me your dreams."

The butler said, "I saw a three-branched vine, with ripe grapes which I pressed into Pharaoh's cup. And then I put the cup into his hand."

Joseph said to him, "This is the meaning of your dream: within three days you will put Pharaoh's cup into his hand once more."

Now the baker told his dream, "I was carrying three white baskets on my head, and in the top basket were many loaves of bread for Pharaoh; and the birds came and were eating them up."

"This is the meaning of your dream," said Joseph: "Within three days you will be hanged on a tree, and birds will devour you."

And so it came to pass. On the third day after that, Pharaoh recalled the butler to his place and had the baker hanged.

Two years later, the butler heard Pharaoh complaining of strange dreams which not one of his astrologers or magicians could interpret. And the chief butler said, "I remember a young Hebrew in the prison who interpreted a dream for me; and all that he said came true."

Then Pharaoh brought Joseph out of prison and said, "Joseph, I have dreamed a dream and no one can interpret it. I saw seven fat cows grazing in a meadow beside the river; and seven thin, ill-favored cows came and ate them up. But afterwards the ill-favored cows were just as thin as ever. And I saw

seven good full ears of wheat that were eaten by seven dry and withered ears."

Joseph said, "God is showing to Pharaoh what he is about to do. There will be seven years of plenty in Egypt; these are the fat cows and good grain. The lean cattle and withered grain are seven years of famine to come after.

"Let Pharaoh find a wise and capable man to store up grain during the seven good years, and provide for the seven poor years to come."

Then Pharaoh said, "Since God has shown you these things, you must be that wise and capable man." He took off his own ring and put it on Joseph's finger, and dressed him in fine linen and put a gold chain around his neck and had him ride in the second chariot. And he made him ruler over all Egypt.

Joseph's Canal in Egypt

Now indeed for seven years there were bountiful crops in Egypt, and Joseph stored up grain every year. So, when seven years of drought followed, there was food for the Egyptians and food to sell to the people of other lands.

It was Joseph who had charge of selling the grain to those who came, driven by famine, from every country on earth.

And it was to Joseph there came ten men from Canaan, who bent very low before him. He knew at once they were his brothers, and remembered how they had bowed down to him in his boyhood dreams.

But so they should not know him, he asked in a gruff voice, "Where do you come from?" When they said, "From Canaan;" he cried out, "You are spies! You have come to spy on our land!"

Egyptian temple existing in Joseph's time

Then to prove their innocence they told him of their home in Hebron and of their father, and of a lost brother, and of the youngest, still at home.

"By the life of Pharaoh," said Joseph, "you shall prove this! Leave one of your number here in prison and do not come to me again without your youngest brother."

Now they said to one another, "We are guilty, because of what we did to Joseph. We saw the agony of his soul when he plead for mercy, and we would not hear him. This is why such punishment has come to us."

They did not know that Joseph understood every word they said, for he had spoken to them through an interpreter.

Now Joseph turned away to hide his tears from them. Then he returned to his brothers once more, and took Simeon and bound him before their eyes.

Then he gave orders that their sacks should be filled with grain.

And they packed their donkeys with the grain sacks, and set off on their journey. But that night at

Joseph recognizes his brothers

the inn, one of them opened his sack, and found lying inside it the very money he had paid for it in Egypt. "What has God done to us?" they said in dismay.

When they reached home each man found his money in his sack. Then they told their father how the governor of that country had ordered them to bring their youngest brother to Egypt.

"Joseph is lost, Simeon is lost, and now you will take away Benjamin, my youngest!" cried Jacob. "No, he shall not go."

But when the grain was all eaten, and they were in dire want, Jacob said to his sons, "Go down again to Egypt, and buy food for us. "We cannot," Judah answered. "The man said we should never see his face again if we did not bring Benjamin to him. But we must have food for ourselves and our little ones. Let Benjamin go, and if I do not bring him back I will bear the blame for ever."

Scene in Hebron, home of Jacob

At last their father Israel consented. "If I am bereft of my children, I am bereft! But I pray God the man will have pity, and give me back Simeon and Benjamin. Take honey and spices and nuts, and double the money. And take the money found in your sacks, for it may have been a mistake."

Thus Israel's sons came again to Joseph. And they were invited to dine at his house.

Now the brothers were afraid of being taken into slavery, because of the money they had found in their sacks, and they stopped at the door and told their fears to the chief steward.

Hebron, among the olive groves

"Peace be to you, have no fear," he said, "I received your money. God must have given you what was in your sacks." And he gave them water to wash their feet and food for their donkeys, and brought Simeon to them.

As Joseph came in they bowed to the ground and presented their gifts.

But when he saw Benjamin his heart was full. "God be gracious unto you, my son," he said, and hurried away to his own room, and wept. Then mastering himself, he washed his face and came in again to the feast with his brothers.

And Joseph said to the steward, "Fill the sacks and put the money inside as before. And in the sack that belongs to the youngest, put not only his money but my own silver cup."

As soon as the morning was light the men set off again. They were not far from the city when they saw Joseph's steward coming after them. "Why have you returned evil for good?" he asked. "Why have you stolen my master's silver cup?"

"You must be mistaken," they answered, "We could not do such a thing! We brought back the money we found in our sacks the last time. Why should we steal silver or gold? Search us, and if it is found we will be your slaves." So all their sacks were taken off the donkeys, and searched, one by one.

And the cup was found in Benjamin's sack.

Now indeed they were dismayed, and they packed their donkeys and went back to Joseph.

They bowed to the ground before him.

"What is this you have done?" said he. "Did you not know I can read thoughts?"

"What shall we answer?" said Judah, "God knows we are guilty men. There is nothing for us all but to be your slaves."

And Joseph said, "God forbid. Only the one in whose sack the cup was found shall be my servant."

Then Judah came near and said in a low voice, "Have mercy, my lord. We have brought the boy, though we thought our father would die of grief at parting with him. For there was another son, who is no more, and this is the youngest boy. I said to my father that I would take the blame if Benjamin did not return to him.

"If we go back without the lad our father will die of sorrow. Let me be your slave instead, and let Benjamin go with the rest."

At last Joseph could bear no more.

"Have all the attendants leave us!" he said.

And he stood alone with his brothers, and wept aloud.

"I am Joseph," he said. "Come near to me," for he saw that the men were afraid. "Do not be angry with yourselves that you sold me. Truly it was God who sent me here to preserve life. For the drought has lasted only two years, and there will be five years more when you will need bread for all your families.

"Go quickly to my father and say to him, 'Your son Joseph who by God's will is governor of Egypt says, Come to me! Do not delay, but come! Bring your children and your flocks and herds, and you shall have the fertile land of Goshen and be near to me.' "

He kissed all his brothers and talked with them and sent them home laden with gifts.

And when Jacob their father heard that Joseph was ruler of Egypt, his heart stood still, for he

View in the Fayoum, Egypt

could not at first believe it. Then he said, "It is enough. Joseph is alive; I will go and see him before I die."

So Jacob set out on his journey with all that he had. And when he came to Beersheba he offered sacrifices to his father's god.

And in a night vision God called to him, "Jacob! Jacob!" He said "Here am I."

And God said, "I am your father's God. Do not fear to go down to Egypt, for I will make your children a great nation there. And I will go with you to Egypt, and I will bring your children back again to Canaan."

So Jacob started from Beersheba with his sons and their wives and little ones, in wagons sent from Egypt. For Pharaoh had commanded wagons and provisions to be sent them for their journey.

Then Joseph got into his chariot and went to meet his father on the way, and embraced him and kissed him and wept over him. And the sons of Israel lived and prospered in Egypt and became a great nation.

By a canal of the Nile

MOSES AND THE COMMANDMENTS

NOW after many years a new Pharaoh came to the throne of Egypt who had never known Joseph.

He was afraid of the Hebrews, because they had become very numerous and powerful; so he put them to hard labor and made slaves of them. But the more he ill-treated them, the more they grew. Then he commanded that every new-born Israelite boy should be thrown into the Nile.

Just at this time Moses was born, and his mother hid him as long as she could, for he was a beautiful child.

But when he was three months old she laid him in a little cradle she had made of reeds daubed with mud and pitch, and set it among the rushes at the river's edge. And his sister stood a little way off, to see what would become of him.

Soon the daughter of Pharaoh came down with her maids to bathe in the river. When she saw the cradle among the reeds she sent a maid to get it. And when she opened it she saw the child.

The baby started to cry, and the heart of the princess was touched. "This is one of the Hebrews' children," she said.

Then his sister ran up and asked, "Shall I get a Hebrew nurse for the baby?"

"Yes, do so," said Pharaoh's daughter. So the girl went and called the child's mother.

"Nurse this child for me," said Pharaoh's daughter, "and I will pay you." And the mother took her baby and nursed him and brought him up. And the child grew and Pharaoh's daughter took him as her own son.

And she called him "Moses," for she said, " I drew him out of the water."

One day after Moses had become a man, he went out to where his own people were toiling, and saw an Egyptian strike down a Hebrew. Looking this way and that way and seeing no one, he killed the Egyptian and hid him in the sand.

But Pharaoh heard of it, and threatened to kill Moses; so he had to make his escape.

Moses went to Midian and spent many years in the wilderness as a shepherd. And while watching his sheep he came to Horeb, the Heights of God.

There he saw the angel of the Lord in a flame coming out of a bush, and though the bush was on fire it was not burnt up.

"What a strange thing," said Moses, "A bush that is burning, yet not destroyed."

And God called him, "Moses, Moses!"

And Moses answered, "Here am I."

"Do not come nearer," said the Lord. "Put the shoes from off your feet, for the place where you stand is holy ground. I am the God of Abraham and of Isaac and of Jacob. I know how My people are suffering in slavery; I have heard their cry for help; and I have come to bring them into a wide, fertile land, a land flowing with milk and honey. Now I will send you to Pharaoh, for you are to lead My people out of Egypt."

And Moses said to God, "But if I tell the people, 'The God of your fathers has sent me;' and they ask, 'What is his name?' what shall I answer?"

God said, "I AM THAT I AM. So you will say to the Hebrews, 'I AM has sent me to you.' "

And Moses answered, "But they will not listen to me or believe that God has sent me."

"What is that in your hand?" the Lord asked.

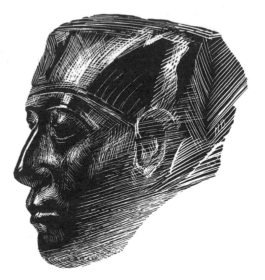

And he said, "A stick."

"Throw it on the ground," said the Lord. And when the stick touched the ground it became a serpent, and Moses ran from it.

"Put out your hand," said the Lord, "and take it by the tail." So Moses caught hold of it, and it became a stick again.

And then God said, "Put your hand under your cloak." Moses put his hand under his cloak, and when he took it out it was white as snow with leprosy.

"Now put your hand into your bosom again," said the Lord. Moses put in his hand and it became healthy as before.

And God said, "If they do not believe your words, they will believe these signs that you show."

So Moses with his brother Aaron gathered together all the chief men of Israel, and told them all that the Lord had said to Moses, and showed them the signs and wonders. And the people believed: and when they heard how the Lord had seen their woes and pitied them, they bowed their heads in reverence.

Then Moses and Aaron went to Pharaoh and told him: "The Lord God of Israel says, 'Let My people go, so that they may worship Me in the wilderness.' "

"Who is the Lord?" said Pharaoh; "Why should I obey Him and let the Hebrews go?" And he made their work harder than before. "They have not enough to do," said he, "That is why they ask to go out and sacrifice to their God."

That same day he ordered them to make bricks without straw, and had them cruelly beaten because they could not do it.

The Israelites came to Moses and Aaron, and said, "God punish you for putting a sword in Pharaoh's hand to kill us!"

And Moses returned to the Lord; "Why was I sent to these people, O Lord? For since I spoke to Pharaoh he has tormented them, and You have not delivered Your people at all."

Then God said to Moses, "You shall see what I will do. Pharaoh will set them free, — yes, and drive them out. Now tell Pharaoh to let my people go."

"But Pharaoh will not listen to me," said Moses.

The Lord said, "I have made you a god to Pharaoh, and Aaron shall be your prophet. Say to Pharaoh, 'Let my people go!'"

So Moses and Aaron went again to Pharaoh: and Aaron threw his stick on the ground, to show the power of God, and the stick became a serpent.

Then Pharaoh called for his magicians and sorcerers; and with magic art each man threw down his stick and turned it into a serpent. And Aaron's stick swallowed them all.

But Pharaoh's heart was hard. And he would not free the children of Israel.

God said to Moses, "Tell Aaron to stretch out his hand with his stick over the streams and rivers and ponds of Egypt, and bring frogs up over the land of Egypt."

And as Aaron did so, swarms of frogs came out of the water and poured over the land, into the houses and beds and even into the ovens and kneading troughs.

"Ask the Lord to take away the frogs and I will let your people go!" said Pharaoh.

But when the frogs had disappeared he would not set the Hebrews free.

"Rise up early in the morning," the Lord said to Moses; "Go to Pharaoh and say to him, 'The God of the Hebrews says, Let My people go, or I will send all My plagues on you!'"

Moses held out his stick, and there came a storm of hail, and lightning that ran along the ground,

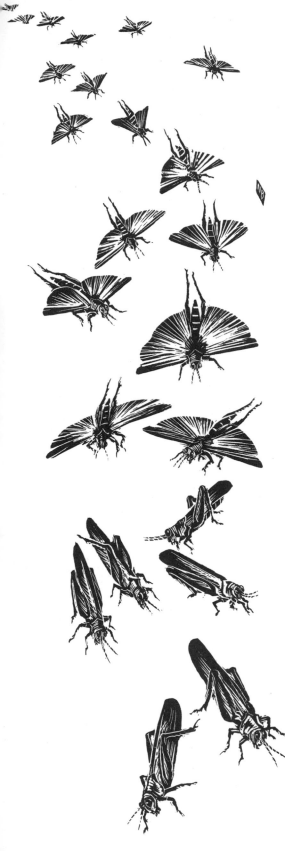

such as had never been seen in the land of Egypt since it became a nation.

All the crops and growing things in Egypt were destroyed, except in Goshen, where the Hebrews lived.

And Pharaoh called for Moses and Aaron. "I have sinned this time," he said; "The Lord is righteous, and I and my people are wicked. Ask Him to stop the hail, and I will let you go."

But when the hail had stopped he changed his mind again and would not set them free.

Now Pharaoh's men said, "Let them go and worship their God. Cannot you see that Egypt is being destroyed?"

"Then go and serve your God!" said Pharaoh to Moses. "But how many are to go?"

And Moses said, "Young and old, all of us, with our flocks and herds, for we must use them in the

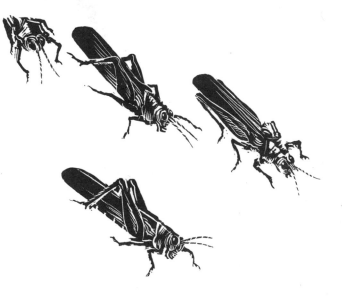

service of the Lord our God."

"Not so," Pharaoh said, and he had Moses driven from his presence.

Moses now held out his stick, and an east wind brought a cloud of locusts over Egypt, eating every green thing that was left after the hail. The ground was black with locusts.

Pharaoh said, "Go, and take your children with you. Only leave your cattle behind."

"Our cattle must go with us," said Moses. "Not a hoof is to be left behind. For we must use them in the service of the Lord."

"Out of my sight!" said Pharaoh. "Never let me see your face again, or you shall die."

Moses said, "You have spoken well; you shall never see my face again. But death shall strike the eldest son of every Egyptian and all the first-born of their animals; while the Hebrews shall be safe. Not even a dog shall snarl at them. For the Lord judges

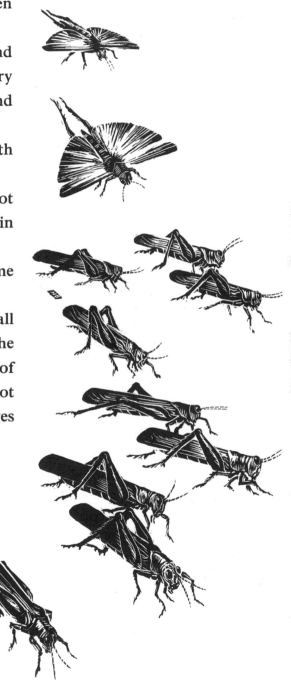

between the Egyptians and the Israelites."

Moses said to Israel, "Let each family kill a lamb, and put some of its blood on the door-posts of the house. You shall roast it, and eat it in haste, with your stick in hand, ready for flight. This is the Lord's passover."

That night the Lord passed over the houses where there was blood on the door-posts; but death struck down the first-born of all Egyptians, from Pharaoh's oldest son to the child of his slave, and the first of all their cattle. And a bitter cry went up in Egypt, for there was not a house that had not one dead.

And in the night Pharaoh called for Moses and Aaron. "Go!" cried Pharaoh, "Leave the country! you and your children and your flocks, — and serve your God!" Now the Egyptians were in such haste to have the Hebrews go, that they gave them silver and gold and clothing and whatever they desired.

Thus the people went out, carrying their bread which had not had time to rise. And on the way they baked the loaves of unleavened bread.

And there went out in that night six hundred thousand men, descended from the seventy who came into Egypt with their father Jacob.

The Lord led them towards the desert and the Red Sea, going before them in a cloud by day, and a pillar of fire by night.

But when Pharaoh and his men saw that the Israelites were gone they said to themselves, "What have we done! We have freed our slaves!"

And Pharaoh took his chariots and horsemen and galloped after the Hebrews. And when they saw this great army coming after them, the Hebrews were in mortal terror. "Were there no graves in Egypt?" they cried to Moses, "Must you bring us here to die in the wilderness?"

And Moses said to the people, "Do not be afraid. Stand still, and see how the Lord will save you. For the Egyptians you have seen today, you shall not see them again, forever."

And Moses stretched out his hand over the sea, and the Lord made the sea divide by a strong east wind all that night, and the waves rolled away to either side. So the Israelites crossed the Red Sea on dry ground.

Then the Egyptians went in after them, horsemen, chariots, horses, and all.

The Lord said to Moses: "Lift up your hand and bring the water back again." And the water came rushing back and covered the horses and the chariots and the men, till there was not so much as one of them left.

Now the Hebrews went three days in the desert without water. And when they found water it was so bitter they could not drink it. "What are we to drink?" they groaned. Then God showed Moses a plant which made the water sweet.

Soon they found a place with palm trees and plenty of good water, and here they rested.

Again they set out across the wilderness. But they kept saying, "If only we had died in Egypt, instead of starving here! We remember the fish we used to have, the cucumbers and the melons and the leeks and the onions and the garlic. Now who will give us any meat in this desert?"

The Lord said to Moses, "I will rain food from heaven for you. And you shall know that I am the Lord your God."

That very evening, quails came up and fell in heaps all around the camp. And the next day on the face of the desert there were small round things that covered the ground like frost.

The people, not knowing what it was, called it "manna." ("What is this?") "This is bread sent from God," said Moses. They found it tasted like wafers made with honey. So they gathered it, some more, some less. And when they measured it out they had enough for all.

"Do not leave any!" Moses warned them. But some of the people kept it until the next day, and it spoiled during the night. So each morning they took

up just enough of the manna for that day.

On the sixth day they gathered twice as much, to provide for the Sabbath, and it did not spoil, but stayed fresh and good.

"There will be none to gather on the Sabbath," said Moses. And in fact, if anyone went to look for manna on that day, he found none.

This was their bread for forty years, until they came to the Promised Land.

Through heat and cold they travelled on, thirsty and weary often, hopeful at times and despairing at times; yet their bodies were strong, and their clothes

did not wear out, all the while they were wandering in the desert.

Now they came near Mount Sinai.

Moses went up to the mountain, and the Lord spoke: "Say this to the Israelites, 'You have seen what I did to the Egyptians, and how I carried you on eagles' wings, and brought you to myself. For all the earth is Mine. Now therefore if you will obey My voice, and keep faith with Me, you shall be My special treasure, a kingdom of priests, a holy nation.' "

And the people answered, "Whatever the Lord says, we will do."

So Moses brought them out from the camp to the foot of Mount Sinai. And as they came near, all the mountain shook and gave out smoke like a furnace.

Then God called Moses up to the top of Mount Sinai, and gave him commandments written on tablets of stone, and other laws for governing the people. And Moses was with the Lord forty days and forty nights.

The Ten Commandments were these:

I am the Lord, your God, who brought you out of Egypt, out of slavery. You must have no other gods beside Me.

You must not make any image nor bow down to any image.

You must not use the name of the Lord in a wrong way.

Remember the Sabbath, and keep it sacred. You must not do any work on that day, for it is the day

when the Lord rested from His work.

Honor your father and mother, and you will live long in the land God gives you.

You must not kill.

You must not commit adultery.

You must not steal.

You must not be a false witness against your neighbor.

You must not desire anything that belongs to your neighbor.

KING JAMES VERSION

THE TEN COMMANDMENTS, *Ex. 20:8–17*

Thou shalt have no other gods before me.

Thou shalt not make unto thee any graven image, or any likeness of anything that is in heaven above, or that is in the earth beneath, or that is in the water under the earth:

Thou shalt not bow down thyself to them, nor serve them: for I the Lord thy God am a jealous God, visiting the iniquity of the fathers upon the children unto the third and fourth generation of them that hate me;

And showing mercy unto thousands of them that love me, and keep my commandments.

Thou shalt not take the name of the Lord thy God in vain; for the Lord will not hold him guiltless that taketh his name in vain.

Remember the sabbath day, to keep it holy.

Six days shalt thou labor, and do all thy work:

But the seventh day is the sabbath of the Lord thy God: in it thou shalt not do any work, thou, nor thy son, nor thy daughter, thy manservant, nor thy maidservant, nor thy cattle, nor thy stranger that is within thy gates:

For in six days the Lord made heaven and earth, the sea, and all that in them is, and rested the seventh day: wherefore the Lord blessed the sabbath day, and hallowed it.

Honour thy father and thy mother: that thy days may be long upon the land which the Lord thy God giveth thee.

Thou shalt not kill.

Thou shalt not commit adultery.

Thou shalt not steal.

Thou shalt not bear false witness against thy neighbor.

Thou shalt not covet thy neighbor's house, thou shalt not covet thy neighbor's wife, nor his manservant, nor his maidservant, nor his ox, nor his ass, nor any thing that is thy neighbor's.

Now because Moses was so long in returning from the mountain, the people said to Aaron, "Come make a god to lead us. As for this Moses, we do not know what has become of him."

Then Aaron said, "Bring your gold earrings to me." He melted the gold, and from the metal he shaped an image of a calf.

"O Israelites," they shouted, "This is the god that brought you up out of Egypt!"—and they worshiped the golden calf.

"Go down," the Lord said to Moses. "For the people you brought out of Egypt have made a calf of gold and are kneeling to worship it."

When Moses came down the mountainside, and

Jewels worn in Egypt at the time of Moses

Mount Sinai (sketched at traditional site)

saw the golden calf, and the people singing and dancing around it, his anger was hot. He flung down the tablets of stone and broke them at the foot of the mountain.

The golden calf he burned, and ground into powder.

Then Moses said, "I will go up to the Lord again; perhaps I may make amends for your sin." And he went up Mount Sinai once more.

The Lord said to him, "Cut two stone tablets like the first ones which you broke, and I will write on them the very same words."

So Moses stayed forty days and forty nights on Mount Sinai as before, and wrote on the stone the

same laws and the Ten Commandments.

Now when he came down from the mountain his face shone so bright that the people were afraid to come near him; and he had to put a veil over his face while he talked with them and told them all that God had commanded.

At last their hearts were stirred. When Moses spoke of making a shrine for the Ten Commandments, they came bringing their precious stones, their bracelets and rings and earrings and other ornaments of gold as a free-will offering. And they brought silver and brass, and spice and incense and badgers' skins and goats' skins, and oil for the sacred lights.

And expert weavers made curtains for the holy tent, or tabernacle, of blue and purple and scarlet woolen stuff worked with patterns of angels. And for the priests they wove garments of fine linen cloth.

More and more the gifts kept pouring in, until Moses sent word for them to stop.

On the flanks of Mount Sinai

Moses brings the Ten Commandments

Then skilful workmen built the frame for the tent. And they made an Ark, or chest, to hold the Ten Commandments. The Ark was plated with gold inside and out; the poles which carried it were covered with gold, and were held by rings of gold.

On top of the Ark were two angels made of beaten gold, one on either end, facing each other. They bent their heads downward, and they spread their wings toward each other, shielding the holy place.

The incense altar was built of wood and plated with pure gold. Gold and brass were used for the altar vessels, the candlestick, and the dishes and spoons and bowls and sacrificial instruments.

Jewels gleamed in the breast-plate of the high priest, one for each of the twelve tribes of Israel; jasper, chrysolite, crystal, garnet, sapphire, sardonyx, cairngorm, agate, amethyst, topaz, beryl, and onyx.

It was a memorable day when Moses set up the Lord's tent, with its furnishings, and put the Ark in the sanctuary. A bright cloud covered the tent and filled it with the glory of God.

Now the Lord spoke to Moses, saying, "Send out men to search the land of Canaan." So Moses sent the scouts, one from every tribe.

At the end of forty days they returned; and they brought with them pomegranates and figs and a massive bunch of grapes carried on a pole between two of the men.

"We came to the country you told us about," they said, "It is truly a land of good things, and this is the fruit it bears. But the people in it are giant men, and they live in cities that are like walled fortresses. Beside them we are as grasshoppers."

All the congregation cried out, "Would to God we had died in Egypt! Let us choose a captain to lead us back again to Egypt!"

But Caleb and Joshua, two of the scouts that went into Canaan, pleaded with them: "The land we came through is an excellent country. If the Lord is pleased with us, then He will bring us into this land and give it to us; a land flowing with milk and honey.

"Only do not rebel against the Lord, and do not be afraid of the Canaanites. God is with us; He will take us into this good land."

Then those men who had brought the unfavorable report from Canaan died of the plague in the camp.

Only Joshua and Caleb were left of the scouts whom Moses had sent out.

And through lack of faith the people of Israel turned once more to the wilderness.

When all went well, they followed Moses with a good heart, but as before, when the way was hard they turned against him.

Again they came to a region where there was no water, and they called to Moses, "Why have you brought us to such a place? This is no country of wheat and figs and pomegranates! There is not even any water to drink!"

Then Moses and Aaron threw themselves down in front of the Lord's tent.

The Lord said to Moses, "Take your stick in your hand, and call the people together. Then speak to the rock, and it will give water for them."

Moses took his stick in his hand and said to the people, "Hear, you rebels! Must we draw water for you out of this rock?"

Twice he struck the rock with his stick; and water gushed out in abundance, for the people and for all their cattle.

But God said to Moses, "You have disobeyed Me in striking the rock." (For God had told him to speak to it.) "Because of this, you shall not go over with My people into Canaan."

Now when they came to the country lying east of the river Jordan, they had to battle their way through hostile tribes. And Balak, king of Moab, seeing the

Hebrews camped on the borders of his country, was roused against them.

He said to his chieftains, "This horde will lick up everything around us, as an ox licks up grass."

And he called for a wise man, Balaam, and said, "A nation has come up out of Egypt and is spreading over all our land. Come, curse this nation for me, and I will give you anything you ask."

"If Balak were to give me a house full of silver and gold I cannot oppose the word of God," said Balaam; but he went with Balak to the high places of the god Baal, and looked down over the Hebrews' tents lying thick as dust in the valleys.

"How can I curse when God has not cursed them?" said Balaam; for God had spoken to him. "For no sorcery can touch the sons of Israel. I must say what God tells me to say."

"Your tents are favored, O Israel. God has brought you up out of Egypt, and every enemy shall fall before you."

Pagan high place in Moab

At last the people of Israel stood by the river Jordan, at the threshold of the Promised Land. And Moses said to them, "When you have gone into this land of olives and wheat and honey, you shall drive out the inhabitants; and you shall destroy their idols and altars, and wipe out the very name of their gods. And you shall worship the Lord your God.

"Remember how he led you through the wilderness, to test you; and how he fed you with manna to prove that man does not live by bread alone but by every word of God. Do not pride yourselves on taking this country, for it is God who gives you the only power you possess."

Then God took Moses up to Pisgah, the peak of Mount Nebo, showing him the country far and wide, and said, "This is the Promised Land; but you are not to enter it."

A home in the Promised Land

So Moses died on Mount Nebo, a hundred and twenty years old, keen of sight, and full of natural vigor. He was buried on that side of Jordan, though no eye has ever seen his grave.

And the people went into Canaan without him.

When the priests who carried the Ark came to the edge of Jordan, the water divided, and all the congregation went across on dry land.

They came to Jericho with Joshua, their leader. And Joshua commanded the people, "Do not shout, or make a noise, until I tell you to do so. When I say 'Shout!' then shout!"

Only a blast of trumpets was heard that day when the army of Israel followed the Ark and marched once around the city of Jericho.

For six days the silent host and their trumpet call encircled Jericho and returned to the encampment.

And at dawn, the seventh day, they went up and marched around the city seven times to the sound of trumpets. But the seventh time, when the priests blew the trumpets, Joshua said to the people, "Shout! for the Lord has given you the city!" And the people gave such a mighty shout that the walls of Jericho fell down flat; and the Israelites went in and took the city.

And how they gained possession of the rest of the country, and how their children and their children's children lived there, and held to the worship of God, is told in many books.

But in all their history no priest or prophet or king could ever be compared to Moses. For he talked with God; he showed the power of God to Pharaoh; he led the Israelites forty years in the wilderness, and gave the Ten Commandments to the world.

Mount Nebo

Palm trees in Egypt

RUTH AND NAOMI

WHEN the Israelites had conquered the Promised Land and occupied it, they appointed chiefs or judges to govern them.

During the rule of the judges, there was a Hebrew woman named Naomi living in Moab. She had come from Bethlehem with her husband and two sons at a time of famine; and after her husband's death she continued to live there with her sons and their wives, Ruth and Orpah, who were Moabites.

Then both the sons died. And Naomi, bereft of husband and sons, determined to go back to Bethlehem. And she said to Ruth and Orpah, "May God be as good to you as you have been to the dead and to me. You must each return to your mother's house. I have no more sons to give you."

Sobbing and weeping, Orpah kissed Naomi and said farewell. But Ruth clung to her husband's

mother. "Do not beg me to leave you," she said. "Where you go I will go. Where you stay I will stay, your people shall be my people, and your God my God. May the Lord take my life if anything but death shall ever separate you and me."

So Naomi and Ruth made the journey to Bethlehem, and reached there just at harvest time. "Let me go and gather some grain in the fields," said Ruth, "wherever they will let me glean."

"Go, my daughter," said Naomi.

Now the field where Ruth happened to be gleaning was the property of a wealthy man named Boaz, a relative of Naomi's husband. Boaz was coming from Bethlehem into the field, greeting his servants with a gracious word, when he saw Ruth.

"Whose daughter is this?" he said.

"It is the girl from Moab who came back with Naomi," said the chief servant, "she has been gleaning here since early morning."

"Hear me, my daughter," said Boaz, "do not glean in any other field than mine, but stay with my maidens and gather grain along with them. I have heard of your devotion to your mother-in-law, and how you have left your home and your family to come and live in a strange land. May you have a full reward from the Lord God of Israel, under whose wings you have taken refuge."

And he showed her many kindnesses, allowing her to eat and drink with his reapers. And he said to his young men:

"Let her glean among the sheaves, and drop some handfuls on purpose for her to gather."

So she gleaned in the field until evening, and took what she had gleaned into the city.

At night when Naomi saw the grain that Ruth had brought, and when she heard that it was from Boaz' field, she said, "May the Lord bless him! The man is a kinsman of ours. You shall go to him and he will tell you what you are to do."

Quietly one evening Ruth came to Boaz while he was resting beside the pile of harvested grain, and said to him, "I beg you, sir, spread your skirt over your servant, for you are my near kinsman."

"Bless you, my child," said Boaz, "I will fulfill the duty of a kinsman."

So, before the next day was over, Boaz went to the elders of the city and redeemed Naomi's title to her own land, and took Ruth for his wife.

From this marriage came Obed, who was the father of Jesse the father of David.

LISTENING SAMUEL

IN the hilly country north of Jerusalem lived a man named Elkanah who had two wives, Hannah and Peninnah. Hannah had not a child, but Penninah had children.

Now this man went up with his family once a year to worship at the house of the Lord in Shiloh. And

Hill town north of Jerusalem

for the offering there, he gave portions to Penninah and her children, but to Hannah he gave a very generous portion, for he loved Hannah dearly.

Yet Hannah was always grieving because she had no children, and Penninah was not slow in reminding her of it.

"Hannah," said her husband as they sat at the feast, "Why do you weep? why is your heart so heavy? and why do you not eat? Am not I better to you than ten sons?"

Rising from her seat, Hannah went to pray to the Lord. "O Lord," she cried, weeping bitterly, "See the affliction of Your handmaid. Give me a son, and I will pledge him to Your service all the days of his life."

This prayer was answered in due time; for Hannah had a son. She called him "Samuel," meaning "Asked of the Lord."

And that year when Elkanah and his family went

up to offer the sacrifice at Shiloh, Hannah stayed at home with the child.

But as soon as he was old enough to leave his mother, she took her son and went to the house of the Lord.

"This is the child the Lord has sent in answer to prayer," she said to Eli, the priest. "He is to be set apart for the service of God all the days of his life."

So the child Samuel lived at the tabernacle, helping Eli in the priestly duties.

And every year when his family came to worship in Shiloh, his mother brought him a little coat which she had made for him.

And as he grew up there, he learned to serve the Lord.

In those days the voice of God was not often heard, and vision was a rare thing.

But one night after Eli had gone to bed, while the

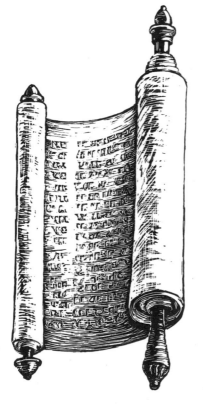

light was still burning in the tabernacle, Samuel was lying awake; and suddenly he heard someone calling "Samuel!"

The boy answered, "Here am I," and ran to Eli, saying, "Here am I, for you called me."

"I did not call, my son," he said, "Lie down again."

Samuel went and lay down; but a second time he heard the call, "Samuel!"

He got up and went to Eli, and said, "Here am I, for you did call me."

Eli answered, "Lie down again, my son, I did not call you."

And the third time Samuel heard the call, he went to Eli and said, "Here am I, you did call me."

At last Eli saw that God had called the child, and he said to him, "Go, lie down, and if you hear the voice again, you shall say, 'Speak, Lord, for I am listening'."

Now the call came again, "Samuel! Samuel!"

This time Samuel answered, "Speak, Lord, for I am listening."

Then God spoke freely, and told him things to come in the future. And when Samuel grew to manhood he became a great prophet and a great judge. He spoke the word of God to all Israel.

"Speak, Lord, for I am listening"

Ancient house, Bethlehem, with sheepcote

THE SWEET SINGER
OF ISRAEL

DAVID was a shepherd boy, tending his father's sheep on the grassy hillsides of Judea.

One day his father Jesse sent for him to come home to Bethlehem. For the prophet Samuel was in Bethlehem, at God's command, to choose a king for Israel from among the sons of Jesse.

First came Eliab, the eldest. When Samuel looked at Eliab, he said to himself: Surely this is the one God has chosen. But God said, "Do not look at his appearance or his height, because I have rejected him. For the Lord does not see as men see; men look at the outside, but the Lord sees the heart."

Jesse called each of his other sons to stand before Samuel, yet of seven sons not one was chosen. And Samuel said to Jesse, "Are these all your sons?" "There is still a younger one," said Jesse, "but he is keeping the sheep."

Then it was that the father called for David, and David came in. He was a handsome lad, ruddy, and good to look at. The Lord said to Samuel, "This is the king: come and anoint him."

So Samuel took the horn of oil and anointed him king of Israel. Strange it seemed, for there was already a king on the throne whose name was Saul. Yet from that time on, the spirit of God came upon David, God's chosen king. Alone with his flocks under the wide sky, he played his harp and sang aloud for joy. And these were his songs:

KING JAMES VERSION

Psalm 23

The Lord is my shepherd; I shall not want.

He maketh me to lie down in green pastures: he leadeth me beside the still waters.

He restoreth my soul: he leadeth me in the paths of righteousness for his name's sake.

Yea, though I walk through the valley of the shadow of death, I will fear no evil: for thou art with me; thy rod and thy staff they comfort me.

Thou preparest a table before me in the presence of mine enemies: thou anointest my head with oil; my cup runneth over.

Surely goodness and mercy shall follow me all the days of my life: and I will dwell in the house of the Lord for ever.

KING JAMES VERSION

Psalm 8

O Lord our Lord, how excellent is thy name in all the earth!

When I consider thy heavens, the work of thy fingers, the moon and the stars, which thou hast ordained.

What is man, that thou art mindful of him? and the son of man, that thou visitest him?

For thou hast made him a little lower than the angels, and hast crowned him with glory and honour.

Thou madest him to have dominion over the works of thy hands; thou hast put all things under his feet.

All sheep and oxen, yea, and the beasts of the field; the fowl of the air, and the fish of the sea, and whatsoever passeth through the paths of the seas.

O Lord our Lord, how excellent is thy name in all the earth!

"When I consider Thy heavens"

Now Saul, the reigning king, was subject to fits of madness, for his heart was far from the Lord. And his servants said to him, "Let us find a man who knows how to play on the harp, and he will play to you and you will be well."

Saul said, "Find such a man and bring him to me."

Then one of the servants said, "There is a fine player named David, a shepherd, strong and manly, well spoken and handsome. And the Lord is with him."

So Saul sent messengers to Jesse saying, "Send me David your son who is with the sheep."

And David came to Saul and stood before him and Saul loved him deeply. And after that, when the madness came David would take the harp and play so sweetly that Saul was refreshed and healed.

There was war in those days between the Israelites and the Philistines. King Saul and his army went out to battle, and with him were the three oldest sons of

Jesse. But David went back to feed his father's sheep.

Facing each other across a deep ravine the two armies were ready for battle, when out of the enemy encampment came a ten-foot giant named Goliath of Gath. He was covered with bronze armor, a coat of mail that weighed two hundred pounds, a bronze helmet for his head, plates of armor on his legs, and a bronze javelin at his shoulder. The shaft of his spear was like a weaver's beam, and its head weighed twenty five pounds.

And he stood and called to the armies of Israel, "Choose a man for you and let him come down to me. I defy the armies of Israel this day. Give me a man, so that we may fight together!"

In Bethlehem, Jesse said to David, "Take this roasted grain and these loaves of bread to your brothers, and these ten cheeses for their captain. Run to the camp and find out how they are."

David was up early the next morning, and leaving

his sheep in the care of a shepherd, he found his way to the field of battle. Out came Goliath, shouting as before, "I defy you, Israelites! Give me a man, so that we may fight together."

"Who is this unholy Philistine that he should defy the armies of the living God?" David asked. And he kept asking the same question over and over until Saul heard of it and sent for him.

"Do not be afraid of this Philistine," said David, "I will go and fight with him."

"You are only a youth," said Saul, "and he is a man of war since his youth."

David answered, "I once killed a lion that was carrying away one of my lambs, and another time I killed a bear. Surely the Lord who saved me from the paw of the lion and of the bear will save me from this Philistine."

And Saul said to David, "Go, and the Lord be with you!"

So David took his shepherd's stick and his sling in his hand, and chose five smooth stones out of the brook and went to meet Goliath.

The giant was coming forward to meet his enemy. A shield-bearer was marching in front of him. All at once he looked around and saw coming towards him a fair red-haired boy.

"Am I a dog, that you come to me with sticks?" he roared, and cursed David by his gods. "Come and I will give your flesh to the birds of the air and the wild beasts of the field!"

Then David said, "You come to me with a sword and with a spear and with a shield; but I come to you in the name of the God of Israel whom you have defied."

Then the boy took a stone and put it in his sling, and struck Goliath in the forehead, so that he fell to the ground.

With a sling and a stone he killed the giant: there was no sword in David's hand.

Many were David's songs of rejoicing:

KING JAMES VERSION

Psalm 46

God is our refuge and strength, a very present help in trouble.

Therefore will not we fear, though the earth be removed, and though the mountains be carried into the midst of the sea.

Though the waters thereof roar and be troubled, though the mountains shake with the swelling thereof. Selah.

The heathen raged, the kingdoms were moved; he uttered his voice, the earth melted.

The Lord of hosts is with us; the God of Jacob is our refuge. Selah.

He maketh wars to cease unto the end of the earth; he breaketh the bow, and cutteth the spear in sunder; he burneth the chariot in the fire.

Be still, and know that I am God: I will be exalted among the heathen, I will be exalted in the earth.

Then David was given a place of honor among the fighting men of Israel.

And all the people loved David. And Jonathan, the king's son, stripped off his robes and put them on David, and gave him his sword and bow, for he loved him as his own soul.

But when the king heard everyone singing David's praises, and when he saw how wise and gentle and fearless the young man was, and how well he carried out every task assigned to him, Saul knew that God was with David.

And Saul feared for his throne. So he made up his mind to kill David. And when David came to play on the harp, Saul threw his spear at him.

Wilderness of Judea

Twice David avoided the spear, and then he fled into the night. Saul said, "He shall surely die."

It was Jonathan who helped David to escape. "Hide in the field and wait for three days," said Jonathan, "and if the danger is over I will shoot an arrow to this side of the stone-heap you see there. But if you hear me say to the little lad that carries my arrows, 'The arrow is beyond you!' you will know that there is danger; you must be off and away."

On the third day David heard Jonathan calling to his little lad, "The arrow is beyond you. Be quick! Do not delay!" Then David knew that the king's anger had not gone down, and he made for the wilderness.

Wilderness of Moab

And in the wilderness David's brothers and kinsmen, and many who were discontented or in trouble, came and stayed with him; and they chose him their captain.

Now Saul and his men set out over the cliffs, through the deep gorges, night and day, searching for David. And when they came to the Wild Goat Hills, Saul went into a cave to rest.

But this cave was the very place where David and his men were in hiding. And while Saul was resting there, David came quietly up and cut off the end of the king's robe.

As Saul left the cave, David called out from a distance, "My lord the king! See this piece of your robe I have cut off! Could not I have killed you? Truly I will not lay my hand on you."

Then Saul wept and said, "O my son David, you are a better man than I. You have returned good for evil; now I know that you will be king of Israel."

Yet Saul did not stop his pursuit of David. And at another time, when the king was asleep surrounded by his soldiers in an encampment on the hill of Hachilah, David came and carried off his spear and water jug. Not a man awoke, for a deep sleep sent by the Lord had fallen on them. And from a hill some distance away, he called, "Why have you not guarded your king? See his spear and his jug of water! When you hunt me, it is as if you were chasing a flea or a partridge in the mountains!"

But the Philistines came again to fight with Israel in deadly combat. Many brave men were slain, even Jonathan, the king's heir, and two of his brothers. And when the king, wounded and despairing, saw the battle going against him, he pleaded with his

own armor-bearer to run him through with a sword. But the armor-bearer would not, for he was afraid. Then Saul fell on his sword and killed himself.

And the men of Israel left their villages and fled, and the Philistines came and lived in the villages.

Then in their hour of defeat all the tribes of Israel called David to be their leader. And he was anointed king over Israel. He laid siege to Jerusalem, and took it for his stronghold. And he brought the Ark of the Lord into the city on a new cart, with shouting and dancing and with the sound of the trumpet. Thus he established his rule in Jerusalem.

And David rebuilt the city, making new walls and towers and courts and palaces, so that Jerusalem in her beauty and security became for the Children of Israel a holy place, and for all nations of the world a name and symbol of that eternal City of God towards which the eyes of men must ever turn. Many songs have been sung in praise of the City of Zion:

KING JAMES VERSION

Psalm 125

As the mountains are round about Jerusalem, so the Lord is round about his people from henceforth even for ever.

Psalm 48

Beautiful for situation, the joy of the whole earth, is mount Zion, on the sides of the north, the city of the great King.

Let mount Zion rejoice, let the daughters of Judah be glad, because of thy judgments.

Walk about Zion, and go round about her: tell the towers thereof.

Mark ye well her bulwarks, consider her palaces.

Psalm 50

Out of Zion, the perfection of beauty, God hath shined.

Now in all the country there was no one so handsome as the king's son Absalom. From the soles of his feet to his magnificent crown of hair, there was no defect in him. But Absalom wished to have his father's kingdom.

"Oh, if I were only judge in this land!" he said to the people, "I would give every man a fair chance!" With flattery and promises of rich reward he stole away their hearts; and at last he raised an army against the king.

To avoid a battle with his son in Jerusalem, David left the city, and went barefoot and weeping up Mount Olivet. And all those who were with him wept as they went along.

In the wood of Ephraim the soldiers of Absalom fought against the soldiers of the king. And the king said, "Deal gently with the young man Absalom!"

But as Absalom was riding a mule through the

forest he went under a great oak tree, and Absalom's head caught fast in the thick boughs; and while the mule dashed away, the rider was left dangling between earth and sky. There the king's soldiers found him, and killed him.

A man came running with news of the battle. He called to the king, "All is well." And the king asked, "Is the young man Absalom safe?"

A second runner came to tell of victory. And the king said, "Is the young man Absalom safe?"

When he learned that his son was dead, the king covered his face and cried aloud in bitter grief, "O my son Absalom, would God I had died for you. O Absalom, my son, my son!"

Then the men of Judah brought David back again to Jerusalem. And in his faith he found comfort and consolation.

From his heart came songs of gratitude:

Absalom's Pillar at Jerusalem

KING JAMES VERSION

Psalm 91

He that dwelleth in the secret place of the Most High shall abide under the shadow of the Almighty.

I will say of the Lord, He is my refuge and my fortress: my God; in him will I trust.

A thousand shall fall at thy side, and ten thousand at thy right hand; but it shall not come nigh thee.

For he shall give his angels charge over thee, to keep thee in all thy ways.

They shall bear thee up in their hands, lest thou dash thy foot against a stone.

Because he hath set his love upon me, therefore will I deliver him: I will set him on high, because he hath known my name.

With long life will I satisfy him, and show him my salvation.

SOLOMON IN HIS GLORY

KING SOLOMON the son of David loved the Lord.
And he prayed, "O Lord, give me an understanding
heart, to judge this great nation."

And God said, "Because you have not asked for long life, or riches, or victories, I have given you what you ask, a wise and understanding heart.

"And besides this, I have given you what you have not asked, riches and fame and long life, and you will be the greatest of kings."

There came two women and stood in the presence of the king. One of them said, "O my lord, this woman has taken my living child from me while I slept, and put into my arms a dead child that was her own son." And the other said, "No, the living child is mine, and the dead one is hers."

The king said, "Bring me a sword." And a sword was brought.

And the king said, "Divide the living child in two. Give half to one woman and half to the other."

Then the true mother cried out, "O my lord, give her the living child; do not kill it."

But the other one said, "Do not give it to her or

to me, but divide it."

"Give the child to the first one," said Solomon, "for she is the mother."

And when all Israel heard of the judgment of Solomon, they reverenced the king, for they saw that the wisdom of God was in him.

The people were as many as the sands of the sea; and they ate and drank and were merry.

Now Solomon sent word to Hiram, king of Tyre, who had always loved his father David: "You know how my father could not build a temple to the Lord his God, because he was a man of war; but the Lord has given me peace on every hand. Now I am planning to build the temple. For this purpose I am asking you to send me cedar wood from Lebanon, and also some of your own workmen, at any wage you say, for we have no men so skilled in the cutting of lumber as the men of your country."

"Blessed be the Lord this day," said Hiram; "be-

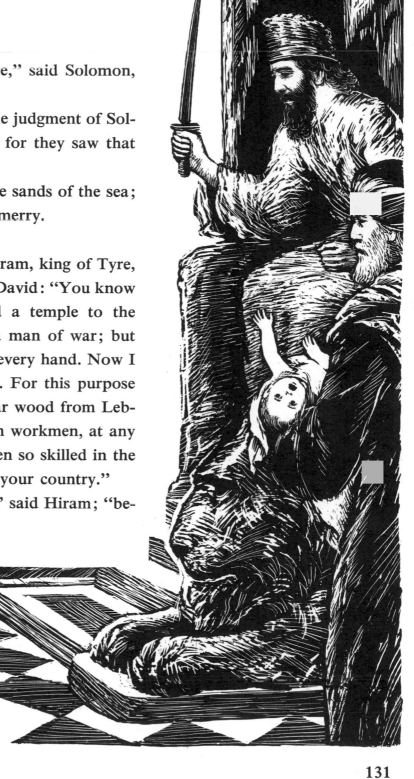

cause He has given David so wise a son to rule over His people." And Hiram cut cedars of Lebanon and fir trees without number, sending them down by floats to a seaport where they were received by the Israelites.

And Solomon had stone-cutters and carriers assembled from all Israel, with officers to direct them. While the stone was still in the quarry they cut and shaped it, so that no sound of axe or hammer or any other tool could be heard while the Lord's house was in building.

Thus they prepared timber and stone for the house of God.

And the temple took shape; with walls and doors and windows, all of stone, and faced with cedar of Lebanon, carved in patterns of flowers and trees and angels. The floors were of cypress wood, the roof was of cedar beams and boards, and the altar was built of cedar.

King Solomon sent to Tyre for Hiram, a worker in brass. Hiram was a master-craftsman; he made columns of bronze for the entrance, and a great bronze basin for storing water, and vessels of gold and brightly polished brass for ceremonial use.

And on the inside of the building, all the walls, floors, and doors were covered with pure gold. The altar was plated with gold. There was a golden chain before the shrine where stood the Ark of the Lord, shielded by two golden cherubs whose wings stretched from one side of the sanctuary to the other. In this Ark were the two tables of stone on which Moses had written the Ten Commandments, when the Children of Israel came out of Egypt.

And it happened on the day when the Ark was set in its place under the wings of the cherubs, that the priests coming out of the holy place were not able to stand and serve; for the glory of the Lord had filled the temple like a cloud.

And Solomon stood in front of the altar of God in the presence of all the congregation and lifted his hands toward heaven and said,

"O Lord God, hear my prayer! Let Your eyes be on this house night and day, on this place which

Giant cedars, Forest of Lebanon

bears Your name. But will God truly live on the earth? for heaven and the heaven of heavens cannot contain Him; how much less this house that I have made!

"Hear the prayer of Your people Israel when they pray in this place. And let all the nations of earth know and reverence You, as do Your people Israel!"

Now after the temple was finished, Solomon had his own house built, of stone and cedar; and also a hall of justice where he sat to judge the people. His throne was ivory and gold; and his drinking cups were gold, — not one was of silver, for silver was common as stone in the days of Solomon, and cedar was abundant as sycamore wood.

Solomon's stables had forty thousand horses, with chariots and horsemen, either in chariot towns or with the king at Jerusalem.

And once in three years a fleet of vessels sailed the seas to bring back gold and silver, spices and sandalwood, ivory and apes and peacocks.

Golden candlestick in the Temple

And people came from all the world to share the wisdom that God had put into Solomon's mind.

When the Queen of Sheba heard of the fame of Solomon, she wished to test him by hard questions. And she came to Jerusalem with a camel train bringing thousands of pounds of gold, and precious stones, and more spices than have been seen before or since.

When she came to Solomon she told him all that was in her heart; and he answered her questions, every one. And when she had seen the house that he had built and his servants and his manner of living, and the way by which he went up into the house of the Lord, she was breathless with wonder.

And she said to Solomon, "The half was not told me, of your wisdom and prosperity. How happy is this nation, and these servants standing always in your presence. Praise be to the Lord your God, who has loved Israel and made you to be their king!"

Solomon's Stables in Jerusalem

Then King Solomon granted her all she asked or desired, besides what he gave her of his royal bounty. So she returned to her own land, she and her camels and her servants.

And Solomon reigned in Jerusalem forty years. He spoke three thousand proverbs and sang a thousand songs, of birds and beasts and insects, and of growing things, from the cedar of Lebanon to the weed that sprouts in the wall.

ELIJAH
THE MAN OF FIRE

AFTER Solomon there came a succession of evil kings who were cruel tyrants and calf-worshipers. But when Ahab the son of Omri came to the throne, he did more evil in the sight of God than all that were before him. For he married Jezebel, a Sidonian princess, and set up in Israel the cult of Baal.

Then there appeared a fiery prophet whose name was Elijah.

Elijah said to Ahab, "By the Lord God of Israel, before whom I stand, there shall not be any dew nor rain in the years to come, except when I say it shall be."

Then God said to Elijah, "You must fly for your life. Hide yourself by the brook Cherith near Jordan. You will have water to drink from the brook;

and ravens will bring you food, for I have commanded it." So Elijah went and hid by the brook, and the ravens brought him bread and meat, morning and evening.

But after a while the brook Cherith dried up because there was no rain in the land. And then God said to Elijah, "Go to Zarephath, for I have commanded a widow-woman there to take care of you."

So Elijah went to Zarephath. And when he came to the gate of the city he saw the woman gathering sticks, and he called to her, "Will you bring me a little water to drink?"

As she was going to bring it, he said, "And a small piece of bread, I beg of you."

"The Lord God knows I have no bread," said the woman, "only a handful of meal in a barrel, and a little oil in a jar; and now I am gathering a few sticks to bake it for me and my son, so that we may eat it and then die."

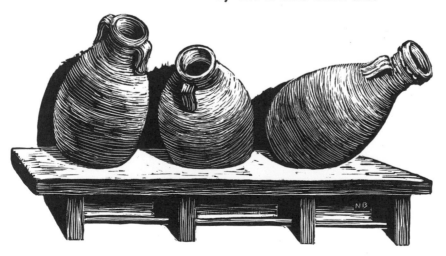

The Brook Cherith, where Elijah stayed

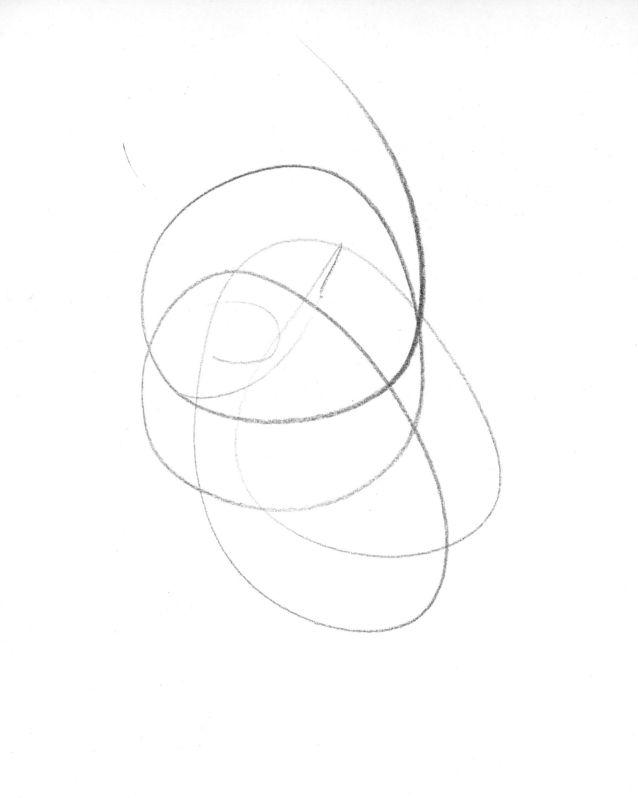

"Do not be afraid," said Elijah, "but go and make me a little loaf first, and afterwards one for yourself and your son. The God of Israel says: The barrel of meal shall not be empty and the oil jar shall not be dry, until the Lord sends rain on the earth."

The woman went and did as Elijah had said, and she and he and all her household had enough to eat for many days. And the barrel of meal was never empty and the oil jar was never dry, as the Lord had said by the word of Elijah.

It happened that the widow's son was taken sick, and became so ill that finally his breathing stopped.

Elijah prayed to the Lord, and the Lord answered his prayer: and the child's life came into him again.

And Elijah took the child, and brought him to his mother, and said to her, "See, your son is alive!"

And the woman said to Elijah, "Now by this I know that you are a man of God, and that the word of the Lord in your mouth is truth."

Gold-covered statue of Baal

After a long time of drought and terrible famine in Samaria, the Lord said to Elijah, "Go now to Ahab; and I will send rain on the earth."

When Ahab saw Elijah coming, he said, "Are you the man who makes trouble in Israel?"

Elijah answered, "I have not made trouble in Israel. It is you and your father's people who have disobeyed the commandment of the Lord and have worshipped Baal. Now gather all the people of Israel together and send them to me on Mount Carmel, with the four hundred and fifty prophets of Baal."

So Ahab summoned the people of Israel and the prophets of Baal, and they gathered together on Mount Carmel.

Then Elijah said to the people, "How long will you waver between two opinions? If the Lord is God, follow him; but if Baal, then follow him."

The people answered never a word.

Then Elijah said, "I am the only one left of the Lord's prophets, but there are four hundred and fifty prophets of Baal. Let them kill and dress an animal for sacrifice and lay it on the wood and put no fire under it, and I will dress another and lay it on the wood and put no fire under it. Then call to Baal and I will call to the Lord; and the god who answers by fire, let him be God."

And the people said, "You have spoken well."

So the priests laid the sacrifice on the wood and called to Baal from morning till noon, "O Baal, hear us!" But there was no answer. And they leaped up on top of their altar.

Elijah mocked at them, "Cry aloud, for he is a god; either he is talking or he is hunting or off on a journey, or perhaps he is sleeping, and must be wakened."

Then they shouted and cut themselves with knives as their custom was, so that the blood gushed out, and kept this up all day long until they were frantic.

But there was no answer.

Now Elijah said to the people, "Come near to me." And all the people came near.

And Elijah took twelve stones for the twelve tribes of Israel, and built up the broken altar of the Lord, making a wide trench around it. Then he arranged the wood, laid the sacrifice in place, and poured on water till it ran down and filled the trench to overflowing.

"Lord God of Abraham, Isaac and Jacob," he prayed, "let it be known this day that You are God in Israel, and that I am Your servant, doing all these things at Your command. Hear me, O Lord, hear me! Let Israel know that the Lord is God, and that You have turned their hearts back to You again!"

Then there came a flash of fire from heaven, consuming the sacrifice, the wood, the stones, and the dust, and licking up the water that was in the trench.

When the people saw it, they bowed to the ground

and said, "The Lord, He is God! The Lord, He is God!"

Then Elijah said, "Seize the prophets of Baal!" And he killed every one of them.

And Elijah said to Ahab, "Now, eat and drink, for I hear the sound of heavy rain."

While Ahab sat eating and drinking, Elijah went up Mount Carmel and threw himself on the ground in prayer. "Go look toward the sea," he said to his servant.

"There is nothing," said the servant.

Elijah said, "Go again seven times."

And at the seventh time, the servant said, "There is a little cloud rising out of the sea, about the size of a man's hand."

Now Elijah said to Ahab, "Prepare your chariot and get down from the mountain, so that the rain does not stop you." But before Ahab could reach his house, the sky was black with clouds. And rain came down in torrents.

When Jezebel the queen heard that all of Baal's prophets had been killed, she threatened the life of Elijah in revenge. But he escaped to the desert.

Alone in the wilderness he sat down under a juniper tree and said, "It is enough, O Lord, take my life now, for I am no better than my fathers." Then he fell asleep.

As he slept, an angel touched him, saying, "Come and eat." And at his side lay a newly baked loaf of bread and a jar of water.

A second time the angel brought him food, and in the strength of that food he went forty days and forty nights in the wilderness until he came to Horeb, the Heights of God.

There he found a cave to shelter him. And he heard the voice of God, "What are you doing here, Elijah?"

And he said, "I have been very faithful to the Lord God of Israel. But the people have forsaken your laws and thrown down Your altars and killed Your prophets. I am the only one who is left, and

Horeb, the Heights of God

146

now they are pursuing me, to take away my life."

And God said, "Go out of the cave and stand on the mountain before Me."

Then came a fierce wind that tore the mountains apart, but God was not in the wind. After the wind, an earthquake, but God was not in the earthquake. After the earthquake a fire, but God was not in the fire. And after the fire came a gentle quiet voice.

When Elijah heard this, he covered his head with his mantle and went out.

And the Lord said to him, "Return now by the desert road to Damascus. Call Elisha to be My prophet; for I still have seven thousand men in Israel who have not bowed their knees to Baal."

Now Elisha was plowing in the field with twelve yoke of oxen when Elijah threw his mantle over him as a sign that he was calling him. Elisha left the oxen, said farewell to his home and his father and mother, and followed Elijah, to become his faithful friend. And they two went on together.

And together they kept the worship of the true God alive through many trials, to be a light for the people of Israel.

When Ahab died, Ahaziah his son became king of Israel. Ahaziah followed in the steps of his father and mother, and served Baal.

At the command of God Elijah rebuked the king for his wickedness. And when Ahaziah sent soldiers to take Elijah prisoner, the prophet called fire down on their heads and destroyed them all.

One day as they were coming from Gilgal, Elijah said to Elisha, "Wait here, I beg you; the Lord has sent me to Bethel." For Elijah knew that the Lord was about to take him by a whirlwind into heaven.

"By the living God, I will not leave you," said Elisha; and they went on together.

At Jericho, Elijah said, "Stay here, I beg you, for the Lord has sent me to Jordan."

And Elisha said, "By the living God, I will not

leave you;" and they two went on. As they drew near to the River Jordan, Elijah took his mantle, folded it, and struck the water. The river parted, this way and that, and they went across on dry land.

Then Elijah said to Elisha, "What shall I do for you, before I am taken away?"

Elisha said, "Let me share your spirit!"

"You have asked a hard thing," said Elijah, "But if you see me when I am being taken from you, it shall be as you wish."

Just as they were walking and talking together, all at once a chariot and horses of fire came between them, and Elijah went up with a whirlwind into heaven.

Elisha cried out, "My father! My father! The chariot of Israel! The horsemen of Israel!"

Elijah was gone from his sight.

Now Elisha tore his own clothes apart and he took up the mantle that had fallen from the shoulders of Elijah.

Courtyard in Shunem

ELISHA THE MAN OF MERCY

THEN Elisha went back to the River Jordan and took the mantle of Elijah and struck the water with it, calling out, "Where is the Lord God of Elijah?"

And the water divided, so that Elisha crossed over to the other side.

The people of Jericho who were standing there said, "The power of Elijah has come to Elisha!"

Now Elisha did wonderful things; he turned a bitter spring into sweet water, and he made poisoned food harmless. And once in a time of famine he satisfied the hunger of a hundred men with a few barley loaves and some fresh vegetables; and when they had finished eating, there was food left over. For the word of the Lord has said, They shall eat and have food to spare.

In Shunem there lived a rich woman who often entertained Elisha at her house. And she said to her husband, "I know that our visitor is a holy man of

God. Let us build him a little chamber on the wall, and put a bed and a table and a stool and a candlestick in the room, so that he can stay there whenever he passes this way."

One day while he was staying in this chamber, he said to his servant, "What shall I do for this woman?"

"Her husband is old," said the servant, "and she is sad because she has no son."

Elisha called her to him, saying, "In a year's time you will hold a son in your arms." And so it was; in a year's time she had a son.

And when the boy was older, one day he was out with his father among the reapers. The father heard him cry, "My head! My head!" and called a servant to carry him home.

And the boy died on his mother's knees.

An upper chamber in Palestine

Then she took him up to Elisha's room and laid him on the bed, and went and called to her husband: "Let me have one of the servants, and a donkey, if you please. I want to go and see the man of God, and I will return immediately."

"Why do you go today?" said her husband; "This is not a holiday, nor Sabbath."

She said, "It is a good thing to do."

Then she saddled her donkey, and said to the young man, "Drive quickly to Mount Carmel." So she came along the road to Carmel.

Elisha saw her in the distance, and said to his servant, "Here comes the woman from Shunem. Run to meet her and ask how she is, and her husband, and the child."

She answered the servant, "All is well."

But when she came to Elisha, she caught hold of him and would not let him go. "As the Lord lives, and as your soul lives, I will not leave you!" she said.

And so Elisha went back with her to Shunem. And there he found the dead boy lying on his bed.

He went in and shut the door behind him and bent over the child, praying to the Lord. After a while the child's body became warm; then he sneezed seven times, and opened his eyes.

"Call his mother," Elisha said to the servant. And when the mother came into the room Elisha said, "Take up your son."

Speechless she bowed to the ground before him. And she lifted up her son, and went out.

Now Naaman, captain of the army of the king of Syria, was a brave man, a mighty warrior, and a great favorite of the king, because by the grace of God he had brought freedom to Syria. But he was a leper.

Naaman's wife had for her servant a small girl who had been brought back a captive by the Syrian troops when they raided the land of Israel.

"If only my master could be with the prophet that is in Samaria!" said the maid. "He would heal him of the leprosy."

The Syrian king heard of this, and sent Naaman to the king of Israel with gifts and a letter asking him to heal Naaman of leprosy.

"Am I God?" cried the king of Israel, "to heal a

man of leprosy! See how he is trying to pick a quarrel with me." And he was wild with fear.

But when Elisha the man of God knew that the king was in distress he sent word to him, "Let Naaman come to me, and he will see that there is a prophet in Israel."

So Naaman came with his chariot and horses and stood at Elisha's door.

And Elisha sent a messenger to him, "Go wash in the Jordan seven times, and your flesh will be restored and you will be healed."

The River Jordan

But Naaman was angry. "I thought he would surely come out to me," he said, "and stand and call on his God and lift up his hand, and cure my leprosy."

"Are not Abana and Pharpar, the rivers of Damascus, better than all the water in Israel? Could not I wash in them and be clean?" And he was going away in a rage.

But his servants came up and said, "Sir, if the prophet had told you to do some big thing, would you not have done it? How much rather then, when he says to you, Wash and be clean!"

Then Naaman went down and dipped seven times in the Jordan, as the man of God had told him to do. And his body became new as a little child's, and he was healed.

And Naaman with all his attendants returned to Elisha and stood before him, and said, "Now I know that there is no God in all the earth but in Israel."

There came a time when the king of Syria was planning to attack the Israelites. But Elisha gave warning to the king of Israel, and saved his life, more than once.

The king of Syria was greatly troubled by this, and he called his servants, and said to them, "Which one of us is on the side of the king of Israel?"

"No one, my lord," said the servants, "but the prophet Elisha tells his king the words you speak in your bedroom."

"Go spy him out!" said the king. "I will send and capture him." They brought word, "Elisha is in Dothan."

So the king sent a company of soldiers with horses and chariots, and they surrounded the city at night.

Early in the morning Elisha's servant caught sight of the warriors and horses and chariots that were on every side.

"O master!" he said, "What shall we do?"

"Do not be afraid," said Elisha, "for we have more on our side than they have on theirs."

And he prayed, "Lord, open his eyes; let him see." Now the young man's eyes were opened and he saw. The mountain was full of horses and chariots of fire, all around Elisha.

So the Syrians went back to their king and never came again into the land of Israel.

THE FIERY FURNACE

IN the reign of Jehoiakim, Nebuchadnezzar king of Babylon came and captured Jerusalem. He robbed the temple of its treasures to enrich the house of his god in Babylon, and carried away the handsomest and cleverest of the Hebrew princes to serve in his royal palace. The youths were to be put in training for three years, given special meat and wine from the king's table, and instructed in the language and learning of the Chaldeans.

Among them were Daniel and three others who were named Shadrach, Meshach, and Abednego.

Animal symbols of Babylonian gods

158

Now the Hebrews could not eat what was served in the palace at Babylon; for to them the Babylonians' food was unclean. And Daniel begged the chief steward to excuse them from eating it. The steward said, "I am afraid of the king, for he will have my head cut off if your face is pale and thin."

Daniel, however, had won the affection of the steward; and he pleaded, "Try us ten days with beans and water."

Finally their wish was granted; and after ten days they were in better condition than all the others who had the royal fare. And therefore the Hebrews continued to eat their own simple food.

Shadrach, Meshach, Abednego and Daniel

God gave them skill in every kind of learning. So when they came for examination they proved to be ten times as intelligent as all the king's counselors. And they were given high position in the government of Babylon.

Nebuchadnezzar the king had set up in the plain of Dura a golden statue ninety feet high and nine feet wide. And he ordered everyone to bow down to this statue at a given signal, the sound of the cornet, flute, harp, dulcimer, and all kinds of music. If anyone should refuse, he would be thrown immediately into a burning, fiery furnace.

Accordingly, when people heard the sound of music, they all bowed down to worship.

But some of the king's counselors came to him and said, "O king, there are certain Jews of prominence in Babylon who do not serve your gods nor bow to your golden statue."

Nebuchadnezzar in his rage and fury sent for Shadrach, Meshach, and Abednego. "Is it true, O Shadrach, Meshach, and Abednego," he asked, "that you do not serve my gods, nor worship the image I have made?"

"O Nebuchadnezzar," said the Hebrews, "we will answer you. Our God is powerful, and he is able to save us from the burning, fiery furnace. But if not, O king, even so we will not worship your gods nor bow to your golden image."

Then the king, full of fury, commanded that the furnace should be heated seven times more than ever. And he gave orders that the strongest men in his army should bind Shadrach, Meshach, and Abednego, and throw them into the furnace.

Now the Hebrews were flung into the fire; cloaks, tunics, headgear, and all. And the fire was so hot that it killed the strong men who threw them into the furnace.

Then Nebuchadnezzar was astonished: "Did not we put three men, bound, into the furnace?" he said; "Here I see four men, walking free and unharmed in the midst of the fire, and the fourth one is like the Son of God."

Drawing near to the mouth of the burning, fiery furnace, he called, "Shadrach, Meshach, Abednego! Servants of the Most High God, come forth!"

So Shadrach, Meshach, and Abednego came out of the fire. And the king's counselors, governors, and captains saw these men whom the fire could not harm. Not a hair was singed, not a garment touched; there was not even the smell of fire about them.

Then Nebuchadnezzar said, "Praise be to God! He saved those who trusted in Him and were willing to give their bodies to be burned, rather than worship any but their own God. Let no one in my kingdom say anything against the God of Shadrach, Meshach, and Abednego."

Unharmed in the midst of the fire

WISE DANIEL

DANIEL was a wise and able magistrate; besides this, he was an interpreter of dreams.

One night King Nebuchadnezzar had a dream which troubled him, but he forgot what it was. When the astrologers and wise men could not remember his dream for him, he flew into a rage and ordered all the learned men in Babylon cut to pieces.

"But why is the king so hasty?" said Daniel; "God in heaven can give the answer." He prayed to God, and God showed him the vision.

Then Daniel came to the king and said, "O king, you saw a huge splendid image with a head of gold, shoulders of silver, thighs of brass, legs of iron, and feet partly iron and partly clay. But a stone cut without hands was hurled at its feet and the great image was shattered to fragments and blown away by the wind. Then the stone became a great mountain and filled the whole earth.

"You, O king, are the golden head of the statue, and its other parts are kingdoms of the future. The stone cut without hands is the kingdom of God, which can never pass away, but will fill the whole earth."

Then Nebuchadnezzar said, "Truly your God is Lord of Lords, for He has told me my dream."

And he made Daniel governor of all Babylon.

After Nebuchadnezzar, his son Belshazzar became king. One day Belshazzar had a feast for a thousand of his lords, and they drank wine out of the golden

cups that Nebuchadnezzar had taken from the temple at Jerusalem, meanwhile singing the praises of their heathen gods.

Suddenly there appeared the fingers of a man's hand and wrote on the wall. The king's face grew pale, his knees shook in terror, and he shouted for his astrologers and wise men. But not one could tell what it meant.

Hearing the uproar, Belshazzar's mother came to the banquet hall. "Do not be troubled," she said, "There is a man named Daniel whom your father appointed chief of his counselors; call him in and he will interpret the vision."

At once Daniel was brought in. And he said, "O Belshazzar, this hand has been sent by the Lord, because you have drunk wine out of the cups taken from His temple, and have honored false gods instead of the God who gives you breath and holds you in His hand.

"This is the writing on the wall; 'MENE, MENE, TEKEL, PERES.' And this is the meaning; Your kingdom is finished, weighed in the scales, and given to the Medes and Persians."

Then Belshazzar gave orders to have Daniel dressed in a scarlet robe with a chain of gold around his neck, and commanded that he should be the third ruler in his kingdom.

But that very same night Belshazzar king of the Chaldeans was killed, and Darius the Mede took the kingdom.

Darius saw the excellence of Daniel, and was planning to make him governor-in-chief.

Now the administration of government was divided between a hundred and twenty princes. These

Kneeling man-headed bull, audience hall of Darius

princes tried to discover some fault in Daniel, that would discredit him with the king. But they could find nothing.

"We shall never find any evidence against this Daniel," they said, "unless it is something in regard to the law of his God."

So they invented a decree that anyone who asked a favor of any god or man except Darius should be thrown into a den of lions. And the king signed the decree, a law of the Medes and Persians, which cannot be changed.

When Daniel heard of it he went into his own house, to his room where the windows were open toward Jerusalem, and kneeled down in prayer as he always did three times a day. And there the princes saw him kneeling in supplication to God.

Then they went to the king and said, "This Daniel, one of your captives, pays no attention to you or to your laws but keeps on petitioning his own God three times a day."

Filled with remorse, the king now set his heart on saving Daniel. All day long he worked to free him;

Daniel kneeling in prayer to God

but the princes came again and said, "Remember that the law of the Medes and Persians signed by the king cannot be changed."

At last the king gave orders to throw Daniel into the den of lions. But to Daniel he said: "Your God, whom you serve continually, He will save you!"

Then they put Daniel into the lions' den, and brought a stone and put it at the entrance. And the king sealed it with his own signet and the signet of his princes, so that Daniel could not escape.

And the unhappy king went to his palace and spent the night without food or sleep. But very early in the morning he hurried to the lions' den, calling out in anguish, "Daniel, O Daniel, servant of the living God, is your God whom you serve continually able to deliver you from the lions?"

"O king, live forever," said Daniel, "The lions have not hurt me, because I was innocent in the sight of God and of my King!"

Now King Darius was overjoyed. He had Daniel brought up out of the den, and issued this command, "Let everyone in my kingdom worship the God of Daniel, for He is the living God. His kingdom shall have no end."

Daniel among the lions

JONAH THE REBEL

THERE was a man named Jonah who heard the voice of God, "Go to Nineveh, the Great City, and proclaim its doom, for I know their wickedness."

But Jonah went instead to the seacoast, and found a ship going to Tarshish. He paid his fare, and went down into it, to get away from the presence of the Lord.

Now the wind blew a gale, so that the boat was in danger of being torn apart by the waves: and the sailors in terror prayed each man to his god, and threw their cargo overboard to lighten the ship.

Jonah, however, had gone below and was lying asleep, when the captain called to him. "What do you mean by going to sleep?" he said; "Get up and call on your God to save us!"

Then the sailors drew lots to see whose evil deeds had brought on the storm; and the lot fell on Jonah.

And they said to him, "What is the cause of this trouble that has come to us? What is your business? Where do you come from? And who are your people?"

And he said to them, "I am a Hebrew. I worship the God who made land and sea." And then he told them he was running away from God.

"Why did you do such a thing?" they said, while the waves leaped higher and higher; "Now what can we do to quiet this raging storm?"

"Throw me overboard," said Jonah, "for I know that the storm has come because of me." So, praying God for mercy, they threw Jonah into the sea. And the wind stopped.

Now a great fish, sent by the Lord, swallowed Jonah; and he was three days and three nights in the belly of the fish. Then Jonah prayed:

"From the depths of hell I cried, and You have heard my voice. You have flung me into the midst of the seas; all Your waves and Your billows have gone over me; seaweeds are wrapped around my head. I am plunged to the roots of the mountains, to the ends of earth.

"When my soul fainted, I remembered the Lord. Now I will offer my sacrifice. I will pay what I owe to the Lord. For God is my deliverer."

Then the fish threw Jonah out on dry land.

And the voice of the Lord came again to Jonah, "Go to Nineveh, the Great City, as I told you, and proclaim its doom!"

This time Jonah went to Nineveh, calling to the people, "Forty days more and Nineveh will be destroyed!"

Now the people listened to the Lord and were ashamed of their wickedness.

The king stepped down from his throne, tore off his robes and put on sackcloth for repentance, and gave this command: "Let every man and beast go without food and water while we implore God to hear us! Leave off the evil things you are doing and the crimes you are planning to do; who knows but God may turn away his fierce wrath and have pity on us?"

When God saw how the people of Nineveh turned from their evil ways, he forgave them and did not destroy their city.

But Jonah was very angry, and he said, "Was not this why I tried to escape to Tarshish, O Lord? I knew Your tenderness and pity; I knew how You put right in place of wrong. Now take my life, for I would rather die than live."

The Lord said, "Are you doing right to be angry?"

Then Jonah went out to the eastward of Nineveh, and built himself a hut where he could sit and watch to see what would become of the city.

Now God made a gourd to grow up over the hut and give a pleasant shade, and Jonah was glad to have it.

But God sent a worm to eat the gourd, and the vine withered; so Jonah was left in the sun and scorching wind, and he said, "It is better for me to die than to live."

God said, "Is it right for you to be angry because of the gourd?"

And Jonah said, "It is right. I am mortally angry."

Then God said, "You had pity on a gourd, that you neither created nor nourished. It grew in a night and withered in a night. Now should not I have pity on Nineveh, the Great City, where there are thousands and thousands of people who do not know their right hand from their left?"

NEHEMIAH AND THE WALL

WHILE thousands of Jews were serving as captives in Babylon, their beautiful city of Jerusalem lay ruined and desolate. How it was rebuilt, Nehemiah tells in his own words:

It happened as I was in the palace of Artaxerxes at Shushan, that certain men of Judah came and spoke to me of Jerusalem, and told me how the wall was broken down and the gates burned away, and the people in great misery.

When I heard this I wept, and prayed, O Lord God of heaven, remember the promise to Moses, If you keep My commandments, I will bring you back from the farthest bounds of earth. O God, give me favor with King Artaxerxes! For I was the king's cupbearer.

Now while I was serving wine to the king he noticed that I looked sad. "Why are you sad?" he asked. "You are not sick; this is nothing but sorrow of heart."

Though I was much afraid, I answered him, "O king, why should I not be sad, when the city of my fathers is lying in ruins, with the gates burned away?"

"What can I do to help you?" he asked.

Then I prayed to God. And I said to King Artaxerxes, "If the king so desires, let him send me to build up the walls of Jerusalem. And give me letters of safe-conduct and an order to the keeper of the king's forest to provide timber for the gates of the wall and the palace and for my own house."

God answered my prayer, for the king gave me all that I asked. So I set off for Jerusalem with the

king's letters and an escort of officers and horsemen.

Now Sanballat the Horonite and Tobiah the Ammonite heard of it, and they were much annoyed that anyone should think of going to help the people of Israel.

When I reached the city, I went out at night and secretly viewed the walls that were battered down, and the ruined gates. Then I approached the chief men and said, "Come, let us build up the wall of Jerusalem." And I told of God's goodness to me and of the king's favor. They said, "We will go and build with you."

But when Sanballat and Tobiah and Geshem the Arabian heard this, they sneered, "What are you going to do, rebel against the king?"

I answered them, "Our God will help us; that is

why we are building. But you have no place, nor right, nor connection in Jerusalem."

So the men of Israel worked on the wall: there were princes, priests, jewelers, shop-keepers, apothecaries, plainsmen, each one in his special place.

At this, Sanballat mocked: "What are they doing, these feeble Jews? Will they fortify themselves? Will they make a wall out of this burned old rubbish?"

And Tobiah said, "What they are building will fall down if only a fox should step on it." (Hear, O God, how we are despised; turn their malice on their own head!)

We continued the wall, joining the parts together, for the people had a mind to work.

As soon as Sanballat and Tobiah and the Arabians and Ammonites and Ashdodites knew that the broken places in the wall were being filled they were

raging, and all joined together against us, saying, "We will steal in among them and kill them and so stop their building."

Even some of our own men said, "We shall never be strong enough to finish the work."

But I said to the builders, "Do not be afraid. Fight for your families and your homes." So, praying to God, we set a watch against our enemies day and night.

From that time, half of my men labored on the wall and half of them held spears and other weapons. Some built with one hand and carried a spear with the other; every man had his sword slung by his side. And the trumpeter was with me, for I said to the people, "If you hear the trumpet, come to help me. Our God will fight for us."

Faithfully we held to the work, guarded by spearsmen from dawn till starlight. Neither I nor my servants nor the guardsmen took off our clothes, except for washing.

When it was known that I was finishing the wall and had left no gaps, though at that time I had not set the doors in the gates, Sanballat and Tobiah sent word to me, "Come, let us meet together in one of the villages in the plain of Ono." But they were planning to do me mischief.

I sent messengers to them saying, "I am doing a great work, so that I cannot come down. Why should the work stop, while I leave it and come down to you?"

Four times they tried to tempt me in this way, and I gave them the same answer each time.

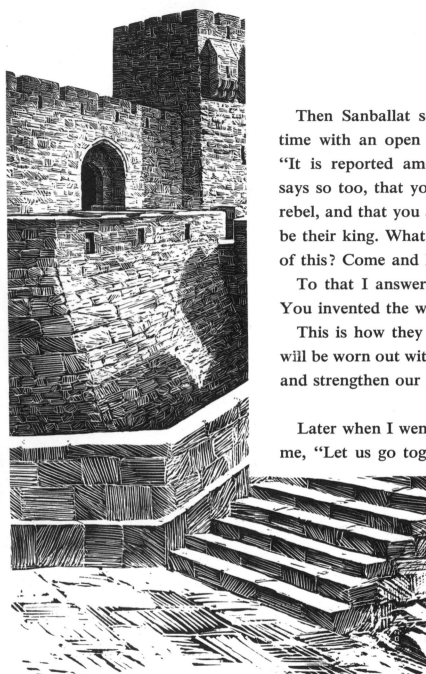

Then Sanballat sent his servant to me the fifth time with an open letter in his hand, which read, "It is reported among the heathen, and Geshem says so too, that you and the Jews are planning to rebel, and that you are building the wall in order to be their king. What if King Artaxerxes should hear of this? Come and let us talk things over."

To that I answered, "What you say is not true. You invented the whole story yourself."

This is how they kept taunting us, "Their hands will be worn out with the work." (Hear this, O God, and strengthen our hands.)

Later when I went to Shemiah's house, he said to me, "Let us go together into the temple, and shut

Tower on the wall

the doors, for they are coming to kill you tonight."

I said, "I will not go." For I saw that God had not sent him. Tobiah and Sanballat had hired him to entice me into wrong.

In fifty-two days the wall was finished. And when our enemies found this was so, their self-esteem had a mighty fall, for they saw it was the work of God.

Now all the people gathered to hear the reading of the law of Moses. They listened with understanding; and when they heard the words of the law, they wept.

But the priests said, "This day is holy to the Lord. Do not weep, or be sad, — for the joy of the Lord is your strength."

The wall of Jerusalem

THE PROPHET ISAIAH

OF all Israel's prophets there was none who had deeper vision than Isaiah the son of Amoz.

He saw the great destiny of his people. Delivered from slavery, trained in the desert, settled in a land of milk and honey, they were torn by rivalries at home and hatreds abroad, yielding often to powerful neighbors and strange customs, yet always returning to the One God. From God must come their Savior.

Isaiah thus foretold the Messiah:

"The people that walked in darkness have seen a great light; they that dwell in the land of the shadow of death, upon them hath the light shined. For unto us a child is born, unto us a son is given: and the government shall be upon his shoulder: and his name shall be called Wonderful, Counselor, The mighty God, The everlasting Father, the Prince of Peace. Of the increase of his government and peace here shall be no end."

THE NEW TESTAMENT

THE LIGHT OF THE WORLD

IN the days of Caesar Augustus, an order was sent out for everyone in the Roman Empire to be taxed in his own city. And a man named Joseph went with his promised wife from Nazareth to be taxed at Bethlehem, the city of David. For they were of the family of David.

There in Bethlehem was born to Mary a child of the Holy Spirit. Mary wrapped her babe in swaddling clothes, and laid him in a manger, because there was no room for them at the inn.

In the fields nearby were shepherds watching their flocks that night. Suddenly an angel of the Lord appeared to them, and the glory of the Lord shone over them. And they were much afraid.

"Have no fear," said the angel, "for I am bringing you good news of joy for all mankind. Today in the city of David is born a Savior, who is Christ the Lord. You will find him wrapped in swaddling clothes and lying in a manger."

All at once there came a host of angels praising God and saying, "Glory to God in the highest, and on earth peace, good will to men!"

The shepherds said to one another, "Let us go to Bethlehem and see this thing that God has made known to us." And they found Mary and Joseph, and the babe lying in a manger.

At the same time, there came wise men from the East to Jerusalem, saying, "Where is the new-born babe who will be king of the Jews?" For we have seen his star in the East and have come to bow before him."

When King Herod heard of this, he was troubled, and gathered together the chief priests and scribes, and demanded of them where the Messiah would be born.

"In Bethlehem of Judea, according to prophecy," they said.

Then Herod called the wise men and inquired of

them when the star had appeared. And he sent them to Bethlehem, and said, "Go, and search for the young child, and when you have found him, bring me word, so that I may do him honor."

When they had heard the king, they went until they saw the star shining over the place where the young child was. There they found the babe, and Mary his mother. They bowed low to worship, and opening up their treasures they presented gifts of gold and frankincense and myrrh. And because they were warned in a dream not to return to Herod, they went by another road to their own country.

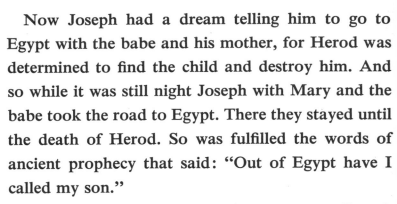

Now Joseph had a dream telling him to go to Egypt with the babe and his mother, for Herod was determined to find the child and destroy him. And so while it was still night Joseph with Mary and the babe took the road to Egypt. There they stayed until the death of Herod. So was fulfilled the words of ancient prophecy that said: "Out of Egypt have I called my son."

When Herod died, another dream came to Joseph in Egypt, saying, "Come, bring the babe and his mother back to the land of Israel, for those who would take the child's life are dead." So Joseph and Mary and the babe came northward again. Now Joseph had been warned against the new king of Judea, who was Herod's son, and he could not stay in Judea, but went to Galilee, and made his home in Nazareth.

The child was named Jesus, "God is salvation." And God's favor rested on him.

When Jesus was twelve years old his family took him to the Passover Feast in the temple at Jerusalem. But when the feast was finished, as they were on their way home, they missed the boy and went back to look for him.

After three days they found him in Jerusalem, talking with the elders in the temple. And everyone that heard him was astonished at his questions and answers, for he understood without having to be taught.

"Son," said his mother, "why have you treated us so? We were looking everywhere for you, and were anxious about you."

But Jesus said, "Why were you looking for me? Did you not know that I must be at my Father's business?"

These words seemed strange to them, for they did not understand the boy. Yet his mother kept all his sayings in her heart.

So he went home, and was obedient to them, and worked with Joseph in the carpenter's shop. And he grew in body and in spirit, beloved by God and man.

Jesus' coming was heralded by John the Baptist, a man who lived in the desert and called people everywhere to repent, be cleansed of their sins, and be baptized in the River Jordan. "For the kingdom of heaven is at hand!" said John. "Prepare the way for the Lord."

Now Jesus came to be baptized. And as he came up out of the water the spirit of God descended upon him like a dove, and there came a voice from heaven saying, "This is my beloved Son, in whom I am well pleased."

Jesus was at this time about thirty years of age. And he went into the desert and was with the wild

Hillside near Nazareth

beasts, and had nothing to eat for forty days. And he struggled with the devil, who tormented him by hunger, and pride, and fear, until at last Jesus cried out, "Be gone, Satan!"

Then the devil let him alone; and angels came and brought him what he needed.

And Jesus returned to his own country strong in spirit, and began to speak to the people:

"Come to me, all who labor under heavy burdens," he said, "and I will give you rest."

"I am the good shepherd. My sheep listen to my voice, and I give them eternal life. They shall never perish, for no one can tear them away from me. My Father who gave them to me is greater than all, and no one can take them away from Him. I and my Father are one."

Calling a little child, Jesus set him down where

A shepherd in Galilee

all could see, and said to them, "Unless you become like this little child, you can never enter the kingdom of God. Let the children come to me, do not keep them away; for the kingdom of God belongs to them.

"Love your enemies, and you will truly be the children of your heavenly Father.

"The kingdom of God is like a rare pearl, a man will sell all he has to buy it.

"But the kingdom of God does not come where

the eye can see it. No one will say, 'Look! Here it is!' or 'There it is!' — for the kingdom of heaven is in you."

And crowds came from all Galilee to hear him, and brought those who were ill or in distress of any kind, and he healed them all, so that those who were dumb began to speak, the lame ones walked, and the blind recovered their sight.

One day as he was passing along the shores of Lake Galilee, Jesus saw two fishermen, Andrew and

Peter, casting a net into the water. "Come with me," he called to them; "and I will teach you to fish for men." At once they left their nets and followed him.

So he called twelve disciples or students to preach the good news of God's care for His people. And he gave these disciples power to heal insanity and every kind of disease, and to bring the dead back to life.

The disciples were first Simon, called Peter, and Andrew his brother; James the son of Zebedee, and John his brother; Philip and Bartholomew; Thomas, and Matthew the tax-collector, James the son of Alpheus, and Lebbeus Thaddeus, Simon the Canaanite, and Judas Iscariot, the one who later betrayed Jesus.

Jesus sent them from place to place through all Galilee, to teach and to heal. And people came to Jesus from Jerusalem, from Syria, and from beyond Jordan. And he went up and sat on a hillside and

Flowers in Galilee

spoke to the throng gathered there, saying:

Blessed are the poor in spirit; for their's is the kingdom of heaven.

Blessed are they that mourn: for they shall be comforted.

Blessed are the meek: for they shall inherit the earth.

Blessed are they which do hunger and thirst after righteousness: for they shall be filled.

Blessed are the merciful: for they shall obtain mercy.

Blessed are the pure in heart: for they shall see God.

Blessed are the peacemakers: for they shall be called the children of God.

Blessed are they which are persecuted for righteousness' sake: for their's is the kingdom of heaven.

Blessed are ye, when men shall revile you and persecute you, and shall say all manner of evil against you falsely, for my sake.

Rejoice, and be exceeding glad: for great is your reward in heaven: for so persecuted they the prophets which were before you.

KING JAMES VERSION
THE BEATITUDES

And as he was praying, one of the disciples said to him. "Master, teach us to pray, as John taught his disciples."

And Jesus gave them this prayer:

Our Father which art in heaven, Hallowed be thy name.
Thy kingdom come. Thy will be done in earth, as it is in heaven.
Give us this day our daily bread.
And forgive us our debts, as we forgive our debtors.
And lead us not into temptation, but deliver us from evil: for thine is the kingdom, and the power, and the glory, for ever. Amen.

And Jesus said to the people "See the flowers in the field, how they grow! without effort, without toiling for their clothes, and yet I tell you Solomon in all his glory was not adorned like one of these.

Flowers of the field, sketched in Galilee

Now if God dresses the wild-flowers in such beauty, surely He will provide clothing for you. How can you doubt?

"And why are you always saying, 'What shall we eat?' or 'What shall we drink?' or 'What shall we wear?' Your heavenly Father knows your need of all these things.

"Look first for the kingdom of God, and His goodness; and all these things will be given to you besides.

"Think of the birds: they never plant seeds or reap a harvest, and yet your Father in heaven feeds and cares for them. Not a sparrow falls to the ground but what your Father knows it. Surely you are dearer to Him than many sparrows.

"Ask, and you will receive. Seek and you will find. Only knock, and the door will be opened to you. For everyone that asks will receive, and whoever

On the road to Nazareth

Bethlehem

seeks will find, and to everyone who knocks the door will be opened.

"Will any one of you who is a father give his son a stone when he asks for bread? or a snake when he asks for a fish? Now if you, evil as you may be, know how to give good gifts to your children, how much more will your heavenly Father give good things to those who ask Him!

"Love the Lord your God with all your heart, and with all your soul, and with all your strength, and with all your mind; and love your neighbor as yourself.

"Do to others as you would like to have them do to you.

"Be perfect, just as your Father in heaven is perfect."

At another time Jesus told them this story:

There was a man who had two sons. The younger one said to his father, "Father, give me my share of the property." And when the father had given him his share, the young man went to a distant country and spent the money wildly until it was all gone.

And when he had spent all he had, there was a severe famine in that country, and he began to feel the pinch of hunger. So he hired out as a keeper of pigs. And he would gladly have eaten the husks they fed to the pigs, but they would give him nothing.

And when he came to his right mind he said to himself, "How many of my father's servants have enough to eat and to spare, and here I am dying of starvation! I will go back to my father, and say to

Nazareth

him, "Father, I have sinned against heaven and against you, and am no more worthy to be called your son. Let me be a hired servant in your house."

So he started homeward. But while he was still a long way off the father saw him and yearned for his son; and he ran to meet him, and kissed him and held him in a strong embrace.

"Father, I have done wrong in the sight of God, and of you!" cried the boy; "I am not worthy to be called your son."

But the father said to his servants, "Bring out the best clothes and put them on him, and put a ring on his finger, and shoes on his feet, and let us feast and be glad today, for this son of mine was dead and is alive again. He was lost, and is found!"

The Prodigal Son is welcomed

And they began to make a celebration.

But the elder son had been out in the field all the while, and now he came near to the house, and heard the sound of music and dancing. "What does this mean?" he asked one of the servants.

The servant said, "Your brother has come home, and your father has killed the fatted calf because he has come back safe and sound."

Now the elder brother was angry, and refused to go in, though his father begged him to come.

"How many years have I obeyed you," said the elder son, "and yet you never even gave me a young goat to eat with my friends. But now that this rascal comes back after wasting all your money, you give a grand feast for him!"

"Son," said his father, "you are always with me, and all that I have is yours."

Now there was a marriage in Cana in Galilee, and Jesus' mother was there, and Jesus and his disciples were also at the wedding. But the wine was giving out, and Jesus' mother said to him, "They have no wine."

He said to the servants, "Fill the water jars with water, and take them to the master of the feast."

But the master of the feast did not know where it came from; only the servants knew. And when he had tasted the water, it was turned into wine.

He then called the bridegroom and said, "The good wine is usually served first, and the less good is served at the last; but you have kept the best wine until now!"

Another time when Jesus was in Cana, a certain nobleman implored him to come down to Capernaum and heal his son, who was dying.

Cana in Galilee

"Unless you see signs and wonders you will not believe," said Jesus.

"Come down, sir," said the nobleman, "before my child dies!"

Jesus said to him, "Go to your home, your son is well." And the man believed, and turned towards his home. On the way, his servants met him, saying, "Your son is well! Yesterday at one o'clock the fever left him."

The father knew it was at that very hour that Jesus had said to him, "Your son is well."

Now it happened one day that Jesus and his friends were going to a city called Nain. Just as they came to the gate of the city they saw a dead man being carried out for burial. He was the only son of a widowed mother. And there were crowds of people from that city following along.

In the city of Nain

When Jesus saw the mother his heart was touched, and he said to her, "Do not cry."

Then he laid his hand on the bier, and the men who were carrying it stood still. And he said, "Young man, I say to you, awake!"

And the man that was dead sat up and began to speak. And Jesus gave him over to his mother.

Now wonder seized them all, and they said, "This is a great prophet!" "God has shown Himself to His people!"

One of the Pharisees or chief men of the synagogue invited Jesus to dine at his house.

And while they were sitting at dinner, a woman of the city came in with an alabaster jar of sweet ointment.

She stood beside Jesus weeping, and as her tears fell on his feet she dried them with her hair, and kissed his feet and poured over them the perfumed oil.

Now the Pharisee who had invited Jesus to dine thought to himself, "If this man were really a prophet, he would have known what sort of woman this is who is touching him. For she leads a bad life."

But Jesus said, "Simon, I have something to say to you."

"Yes, Master," said Simon.

Turning to the woman Jesus said, "See this woman. While you gave me no water for my feet, she has washed them with her tears and dried them with her own hair.

"You gave me no kiss of welcome, but ever since

I came in she has been tenderly kissing my feet.

"You gave me no oil, even for my head, but this woman has covered my feet with perfume.

"This is why I say to you her sins, many though they be, have been forgiven, because of her great love. But if anyone is forgiven little, he is the one who loves little."

And he said to the woman, "Your sins are forgiven."

The other guests began to say to one another, "Who is this man that actually forgives people their sins?"

Jesus said to the woman, "Your faith has saved you. Go, let your heart be at rest."

One sabbath day Jesus went into a synagogue and there he saw a man who had a withered hand.

Now they were all watching him to see whether he would heal on the sabbath day.

And Jesus said to the man with the withered hand, "Step forward."

And to the people he said, "Is it right to do good on the sabbath, or to do evil? to save life, or to kill?"

They had no answer to this.

And when he had looked at them all with scorn, for the hardness of their hearts, he said to the man, "Stretch out your hand."

The man stretched it out; and his hand was as healthy as the other one.

On another sabbath, Jesus was in Jerusalem. And he saw by the pool of Bethesda a sick man who had been lying on a mat for thirty-eight years. Jesus said to him, "Stand up! Take your bed and go to your house."

The man was instantly healed, and walked away carrying his mat with him.

The Temple Area, Jerusalem

Now when some of the leaders of the people heard what was happening, they hated Jesus and threatened to kill him. "He has done such things on the sabbath day!" they clamored, and more than this, "He says that God is his father, and makes himself equal with God!"

He answered them, "Indeed the Son of man is ruler of the sabbath!" and "The Son can do nothing by himself, but what he sees the Father do. The work that I do is proof that the Father has sent me."

Jesus now went with his disciples to the region around Lake Galilee. And throngs of people gathered wherever he was.

One day there came a man named Jairus, who was a leader of the synagogue. He threw himself down at Jesus' feet pleading with him. "My little daughter twelve years old is at the point of death," he said, "I beg of you, only come and touch her, and she will be healed and her life will be saved."

Lake Galilee near home of Jairus

216

While Jesus was going with him, a message was brought from Jairus' house, "Your daughter is dead. Why bother the Master any more?"

But Jesus said to the father, "Do not be afraid; only have faith."

As they came toward the house, Jesus saw a crowd of people there making a great noise, mourning for the dead.

"What is the meaning of all this noise?" he said, "The child is not dead, she is only sleeping."

Then they started to jeer at him, knowing that she was dead.

But he put them all out. Only Peter and James and John and the child's father and mother went with him into the room where she lay.

Jesus took her by the hand, saying, "Get up, my child!"

And before their astonished eyes, the girl began to breathe again, and stood up, and walked.

"Give her something to eat," said Jesus; "And say nothing of what has happened."

Now John the Baptist had been speaking against Herod, the Judean king, and denouncing his wickedness.

Herod had him arrested and thrown into prison, and ordered his head cut off.

John's friends came and took away his body and buried it, and went and told Jesus.

Jesus said to his disciples, "Let us go away to some quiet place and rest awhile." For with so many people always coming and going, they scarcely had time even to eat.

So they took ship and went across the lake to the desert hills, to be by themselves. But people saw them leaving the shore, and many ran on foot to the other side, and were there before Jesus came.

When Jesus saw the host that had collected there, his heart was filled with pity, for they were like sheep without a shepherd. So he healed their sick and told them of God's dominion.

But it began to grow late, and they had nothing to eat in that lonely place. "How shall we buy food for all these people?" Jesus said to Philip, testing him. For he himself knew what he was about to do.

"If we had a great sum of money we could not buy food for them, if each one took only a little," said Philip.

Then Andrew, Simon Peter's brother, said to him, "Here is a boy with five barley loaves and two small fishes; but what are they, among so many?"

"Let the people sit down," said Jesus; and they sat down on the grass, about five thousand persons in all. And giving thanks he divided the bread and fish and handed them to his disciples, who distributed to the people, and they all ate until they were satisfied.

Then Jesus said, "Gather up the pieces that remain, so that nothing is lost."

And they took up twelve basketfuls of what was left from the five barley loaves and two small fishes.

Those who saw the miracle said, "Surely he must be the prophet the world has been expecting to come!"

Now Jesus knew that they wished to take him by force and make him king. So he drew away from them and went back into the hills, to be alone in prayer.

At nightfall, the disciples went down to the lake and got on board ship to cross over to Capernaum. But after midnight the boat was still a long way from shore, tossing on the waves, for the wind was against it.

Toward morning Jesus went out to them, walking on the water.

When the disciples saw him walking on the sea,

they cried out in fear, "It is a spirit!"

"Do not be afraid," said Jesus, "It is I."

Peter said to him, "Master, if it is you, call me to come to you on the water."

He said, "Come," and Peter stepped out and walked on the water towards him. But when Peter felt the violence of the wind he was terrified and began to sink. "Help, Master!" he cried.

Instantly Jesus put out his hand and caught hold of him. "O faint-hearted," he said. "Why did you doubt?"

Now when they had come up into the boat, all at once the wind was still.

The men aboard the ship were lost in wonder and reverence. They bowed at his feet, saying, "You are indeed the Son of God."

As he was coming into Caesarea Philippi, Jesus said to his disciples, "Who do the people say that I am?"

"Some say John the Baptist, some Elijah, and others Jeremiah, or one of the prophets," they answered.

"But who do you say I am?" he asked them.

Simon Peter answered, "You are the Christ, the Son of the living God."

"You are blessed, Simon Bar-Jona," said Jesus, "For this was not revealed to you by flesh and blood, but by my Father in heaven. And I say to you, that you are Peter, a Rock, and on this rock I will build my church; and the forces of hell shall have no power against it. And I will give you the keys of the kingdom of heaven."

Now at the Feast of Tabernacles, Jesus went into the temple at Jerusalem and began to teach. And the people said to each other, "This is the Christ!" But some said, "Is not this the man they wish to kill?" for the priests were determined to get hold of him. Yet no one laid hands on him, because his time had not come.

And Jesus said to them, "I am the Light of the World. Those who follow me will not walk in darkness, but will have the light of life. Your father Abraham was overjoyed to see my day. He saw it and was glad!"

"You are not yet fifty years old," they said to him, "and you say you have seen Abraham!"

"I tell you the truth," said Jesus, "Before Abraham was, I am."

Then they took up stones to throw at him, but he hid himself, and went out of the temple, passing through the very midst of them, and walked away.

In the village of Bethany near Jerusalem lived two sisters, Martha and Mary, and their brother Lazarus.

Jesus loved Martha and her sister and Lazarus, and used to stay in their house. Mary would come and sit at Jesus' feet and listen to his teaching; but Martha was burdened with the housework.

Martha came to him and said, "Master, do you not care if my sister leaves all the housework to me?"

"Martha, Martha," said Jesus, "you are anxious and worried about many things, and yet there is only one thing really needed. Mary has chosen that good thing, and it cannot be taken from her."

Jesus had gone to the other side of the Jordan when the sisters sent him word that Lazarus was sick.

"This sickness will not end in death," he said,

Tower on the wall, Jerusalem

Bethany

"but it is for the glory of God, and it will glorify the Son of God."

Though his friends were very dear to Jesus, he remained for two days in the place where he was staying. Then after that he said to his disciples, "Let us go back to Judea."

When Jesus drew near to Bethany, he learned that Lazarus had been dead four days.

Now Martha heard that Jesus was coming, and she came to meet him. "Master," she said, "if you had been here, my brother would not have died. But I know that even now God will give you whatever you ask of Him."

He said to her, "Your brother shall be alive again."

"I know that he will be alive again in the resurrection, at the last day," said Martha.

Jesus said, "I am the resurrection and the life. Do you believe this?"

"Yes, Master," said Martha; "I believe that you are the Christ, the Son of God."

Now Mary came and bowed in sorrow at Jesus'

feet. And seeing her tears and the grief of friends who stood there, Jesus wept.

And he came to the mouth of the tomb, which was a cave with a stone at the entrance.

"Take away the stone," said Jesus.

"But, Master!" cried Martha, "Lazarus has been dead and in the tomb ever since four days ago!"

Jesus said, "Have not I said to you, Believe, and you will see the glory of God?"

So they moved away the stone. And Jesus turned to God in prayer. "Father, I thank You that You have heard me. I knew that You do always hear me; yet I say this because of the people standing here, so that they may believe that You have sent me."

Then he called with a loud voice, "Lazarus, come out!"

And the man that had been dead came out, though his hands and feet were still wrapped with linen and his face covered with a cloth.

Jesus said to those who were near, "Unbind him, and set him free."

Now the chief priests and elders held a meeting of the High Council.

"What are we to do about this man and his miracles?" they said. "If we let him go on in this way, all the world will believe in him, and the Romans will come and destroy our holy place and our people. It is better for one man to die rather than our whole nation."

After this Jesus could not go about publicly among the Jews, and he withdrew to the desert with his disciples.

But when it was time for the Passover Feast he said to them, "We are going up to Jerusalem, and the Son of Man will be betrayed into the hands of the high priests and elders, who will condemn him to death, and give him over to the Gentiles. They will mock him and flog him and crucify him. But the third day he will come out of the tomb."

The disciples did not understand what Jesus was saying, and they could not comprehend because they did not know the meaning of his words.

On the way, as they came to a village near Jerusalem, he said to two of his disciples, "Go into yonder village, and you will see a donkey tied there, and a colt with her. Untie them and bring them to me."

So the disciples went and found the donkey with the colt, and put their cloaks over her back, and Jesus rode on the donkey to Jerusalem.

And great crowds of people went along with him, throwing their coats on the road, and some cut branches from the trees and spread them in his path. And all the people, those who went before him and those who followed him, shouted, "Hail to the Son of David who comes in the name of the Lord! Glory in the highest!"

And when Jesus came near the city, he wept over it: "If you had only known, this day, the things that are for your peace!"

"O Jerusalem, Jerusalem, murderer of prophets and killer of those who are sent to you! How often have I longed to gather your children as a hen gathers her chickens under her wings, and you would not have me!"

When the disciples were admiring the temple, he said, "The time is coming when not one of these stones will be left on top of another.

"Nation will take up arms against nation; there will be earthquakes and famines; the sun and moon will be darkened and the stars will fall from the sky. Heaven and earth will pass away, but my words will not pass away.

"Be on the watch! And pray constantly to escape from the evil that is coming, and to stand in the presence of the Son of Man."

In the daytime Jesus taught in the temple and at night he went out and stayed on the Mount of Olives.

The people came early in the morning to hear him in the temple. And he said to them, "The priests and elders sit in Moses' place, but though they tell others what to do, they never do it themselves. They put heavy burdens on men's backs, and will not lift a finger to help them.

"Woe to you, priests and elders, hypocrites! You lock the doors of heaven in men's faces, for you will neither go in yourselves nor let anyone else go in.

"You strain out a gnat and swallow down a camel. You are like tombs, white and beautiful on the outside, but inside full of dead men's bones, and all kinds of rottenness. How can you escape the damnation of hell?"

Now that was the time when one of the disciples named Judas Iscariot, knowing that the priests were eager to get rid of Jesus, went to them and said,

Charms and fetishes

230

"How much will you give me if I hand him over to you?"

And they agreed to give him thirty pieces of silver.

From that time on, Judas looked for an opportunity to betray his Master.

On the first day of the Passover Feast as Jesus was sitting with his disciples at the evening meal, he said to them, "I must say this to you: one of you is about to betray me."

And they were very sorrowful, and began to say one after the other, "Master, is it I?" "Is it I?"

"It is one of you twelve, eating here with me," he answered.

While they were having supper Jesus took bread, blessed it, and gave some to each one. "This is my body," he said, "which is given for you; do this in remembrance of me." And afterwards the cup, saying, "This is my blood of the new testament, which is shed for many for the forgiveness of sins.

"Little children, I am with you yet a little while. This is my new commandment to you: love one another as I have loved you."

And they went out to the Mount of Olives. And Jesus said to them, "You will all be put to shame because of me tonight. As it is written, The shepherd will be struck down, and the flock will be scattered."

Peter answered, "Even though everyone should be ashamed of you, yet I will never be ashamed."

Jesus said to him, "Three times this very night, before the cock crows, you will deny me."

"Though I should die with you," said Peter, "I will not deny you."

Then Jesus came with his disciples to the Garden of Gethsemane. "Sit down here," he said to them. And he took Peter, James, and John aside, saying to them, "My heart is heavy to death; wait here and keep watch with me."

He went a little farther on, and sank down in prayer: "Father, if it is possible, take away this cup from me. And yet, Your will and not mine must be done."

When he returned to the three he found them

Gethsemane

asleep. "What, could you not watch with me one hour?" he said. "Now the time has come for the Son of man to be delivered into the hands of sinners. Look! here is my betrayer."

As he spoke these words, Judas came into sight, followed by a company of men with swords and sticks. He went straight to Jesus and said, "Hail, Master!" and kissed him.

The kiss was a signal to the crowd, who caught hold of Jesus and took him prisoner.

At once Peter drew his sword and cut off the ear of the High Priest's servant. "Put up your sword," said Jesus. "Shall I not drink the cup my Father has given me?" And he touched the servant's ear and healed it.

Then he said to the throng, "Have you come to take me like a thief? I sat with you every day in the temple, and you did not lay hold on me."

The disciples all fell back; and Jesus was led away to the High Priest, who had called the Council together.

But in the distance Peter followed him to the High Priest's palace, and went in and sat with the servants, to see what would happen.

Now the priests and elders were hoping to find false witnesses against Jesus, so that they might put him to death. At last they found two men who made the statement, "This fellow said, 'I am able to destroy the temple of God and to build it again in three days.' "

"Have you nothing to say?" the High Priest asked Jesus.

Jesus made no answer.

The High Priest said, "Are you the Christ, the Son of God?"

"You have said it," he answered. "But I say to you, you will one day see the Son of God enthroned in power."

Then the High Priest tore his clothes, and cried

out, "He has spoken blasphemy! You have heard his blasphemy. What do you say to that?"

They said, "He is guilty of death." And they began to spit in his face and to strike and buffet him.

Meanwhile Peter was sitting outside the hall. And one of the maids eyeing him closely said, "You were with Jesus of Galilee."

Peter denied the charge; "I do not know what you are saying."

As he sat warming himself by the fire, another maid said, "This fellow was with Jesus of Nazareth." Again he protested, with an oath, "I do not know the man."

Then the bystanders said, "Surely you are one of them. We know by the way you speak."

Peter began to curse and swear, "I do not know the man."

Immediately the cock crowed. And Peter remem-

bered that Jesus had said, "Before the cock crows, you will deny me three times." And he went out, and wept bitterly.

In the morning Jesus was led to the Governor's Palace. And he stood before Pontius Pilate.

And the mob began to accuse him, and said, "We found this fellow perverting the nation. He says we should not pay taxes to Caesar, and claims that he himself is Christ, a king."

Pilate asked, "Are you king of the Jews?"

Jesus answered, "My kingdom is not of this world."

Pilate said to him again, "You are a king, then!"

Jesus answered, "You say that I am a king. This is why I was born, this is why I came into the world, to be a witness for the truth. Every one that is for the truth hears my voice."

Pilate said, "What is truth?"

And Pilate went out again and said to the people, "I find no fault in him at all." Then he tried in every way to free Jesus.

But those who hated him were insistent: "By our law he must die because he says he is the Son of God!"

And the mob began to shout, "Crucify him! Crucify him!"

When the tumult became an uproar, Pilate called for water and before them all he washed his hands of blame. "I am innocent of the blood of this just person," he said; "See to it yourselves."

And he gave Jesus to the soldiers to be crucified.

They dressed him in a scarlet robe and put a crown of thorns on his head, beating him and spitting on him and bowing down before him as they cried in mockery, "Hail, King of the Jews!" Then they led him off carrying his cross on his shoulders,

to a hill outside the city called Golgotha, the Skull Place.

There they nailed him to the cross.

Beside him were crucified two thieves, one on the right hand and one on the left.

Passers-by nodded their heads at him, and mocked at him, calling out, "If you are the Son of God, come down from the cross!"

And priests and elders exulted; "He saved others, but he cannot save himself."

The earth was dark from noon till three o'clock. Then Jesus uttered a loud cry, "Father, to Your charge I give my spirit."

So he breathed his last.

Now a soldier pierced his side with a spear, to prove him dead. And Joseph of Arimathea, who loved Jesus, came at sunset and took his body from the cross, wrapped it in clean linen and laid it in a new rock-cut tomb. Then he rolled the stone against the entrance and went away. And soldiers came to guard the tomb where Jesus was laid.

Towards daybreak on the first day of the week, Mary Magdalene came and saw that the stone had been rolled away.

She ran to find Peter and John, crying, "They have taken away the Master, and we do not know where they have laid him!"

Peter and John ran to the tomb, and when they saw the grave-clothes lying on the ground they were convinced, and went away again. For they did not yet understand that he must rise from death.

But Mary remained by the tomb, sobbing. Now as she stooped down to look in at the door, someone behind her said, "Why are you weeping? Who is it you are looking for?"

She, thinking it was the gardener, said, "Sir, if you have carried him off tell me where you have put him, and I will take him away."

Jesus said to her, "Mary!"

She turned around to him, "Master!"

That same day at evening, when his disciples in fear of the Jews had locked all the doors, Jesus came into the room and stood with them, blessing and inspiring them with the Holy Spirit.

But Thomas, one of the Twelve, was not there at the time, and when they told him, "We have seen the Master!" he said, "Unless I see and feel the mark of the nails in his hands and the wound in his side, I will not believe."

Again, a week later, Jesus came to the inner room and said, "Peace be with you." Now Thomas was with the disciples. "Put your finger here, and feel my hands," said Jesus, "and put your hand into the wound in my side. Do not doubt, but believe."

Thomas cried out, "My Lord and my God!"

Some time later on, Jesus showed himself to the disciples by the shore of Lake Galilee. Peter and other disciples had been out fishing all night but they had caught nothing. At break of day Jesus stood on the shore (although they did not know that it was Jesus) calling to them, "Children, have you any fish?"

"No," they answered.

"Throw your net on the right side of the boat," he said, "and you will find some."

They threw out the net on the right side; and now they could not haul it in, for the number of fish they had caught.

John, the disciple whom Jesus loved, said to Peter, "It is the Master!"

Peter, when he heard this, fastened his fisherman's coat around him and sprang into the water. The others came in the boat, which was not far from the land, and they dragged the net after them, filled with fish.

There on the shore they saw a small fire already made, with fish on it, and bread. And Jesus said to

them, "Bring the fish that you have caught."

Now Peter got into the boat and hauled the net ashore, full of fine, big fish; and though there were so many, the net was not broken.

Jesus said, "Come and eat;" and he gave them bread and fish.

At another time, while the disciples were having dinner, Jesus came to them and reproached them for their slowness and lack of faith, because they had not believed those who had seen him after his resurrection.

"Go into all the world and tell the good news to everyone," he said. "And these proofs will be shown by all who believe; in my name they will drive out devils, they will speak with new tongues, if they drink anything deadly it will not hurt them; and they will lay hands on the sick and they will recover."

So for forty days after the crucifixion Jesus was seen by the disciples, and on one occasion by more than five hundred of his followers. And then one day, as he was speaking to them of the kingdom of God, a cloud hid him from their sight, and they saw him no more. For Jesus had ascended to heaven.

One day as Jesus was speaking

Now the disciples in great joy went out and preached the good news everywhere; and the miracles that followed were proof that the Lord was with them.

And on the day of Pentecost, they were all sitting together, when suddenly there came a sound of rushing wind that filled the house where they were. And tongues of fire were seen on the heads of all. And they began to speak with foreign tongues, as the spirit moved them. And people of all nations came to hear them, and believed, and became Christians.

And the believers all shared their goods and property with one another in brotherly love.

Once Peter and John were going into the temple, when they saw by the Beautiful Gate a beggar who had been lame from his birth. He called out to them, asking for money.

"Silver and gold I have none," said Peter, "but what I have I will give you." And taking his hand,

Courtyard in Jerusalem

he said, "By the power of Jesus Christ, stand up and walk."

Immediately the man's feet and ankle bones were strong; and he jumped up and began to walk, and went with them into the temple, walking and leaping and praising God. And all the bystanders were speechless with amazement.

"Why are you amazed?" said Peter. "Why do you stare at us, as if we by our own power or holiness had made this man walk? The God of Abraham, and of Isaac, and of Jacob, the God of our fathers, has glorified His Son Jesus, whom you have denied and crucified. Yet God has resurrected him from death: we are witnesses of this. And it is through faith in the power of Jesus, that this man stands before you perfectly healed."

Hearing the disciples speak of Jesus' death and resurrection, the priests and elders were roused up, and had Peter and John arrested and put in jail.

"What shall we do to these men?" they asked one another; for although Peter and John were simple, ignorant people they spoke forcefully and well, and their healing of the lame man had been seen by all Jerusalem and hailed as the work of God.

But no charge could be found against the disciples, and so they were set free, with the command to stop speaking of Christ. Yet they kept on telling the wonderful news.

Time and again the Christians were threatened and beaten and put in prison, but prison doors were opened by the might of God, which broke off their chains and set them free.

Near Nazareth

Roman temple in Damascus

Wherever they went there were miracles and healings. And a throng of believers, both men and women, came to the Lord.

Now certain men of the synagogue were eager to do away with the people of Christ. They stirred up a mob to arrest one of the Christians named Stephen, a man of spiritual understanding and healing power. "He blasphemes against God!" they said. "He declares that Jesus of Nazareth will tear down this holy temple!"

And as they fixed their gaze upon him, Stephen answered them with such ardor that his face glowed like the face of an angel. He told how the hopes of Israel, cherished through the ages, had been fulfilled by Jesus, "But you, stubborn heathen! who have received the law as a gift from angels, you have always killed the messengers of God!"

When they heard this they rushed upon him in a fury and stoned him to death.

Taking part in the scene was a young man whose name was Saul. He had been trained in the synagogue, and with religious zeal he had hunted down the followers of Christ, dragged them from their houses, and thrown them into prison.

Now Saul went to the High Priest, asking letters to the synagogue in Damascus, so that if he found any men or women there who were Christians, he might arrest them and bring them to Jerusalem.

And as he was nearing Damascus, a great light flashed upon him, blinding his eyes, and Saul fell to the ground. Then he heard a voice saying, "Saul, Saul, why do you persecute me?"

"Who are you?" he asked.

The voice said, "I am Jesus, whom you are persecuting."

"Lord, what will you have me do?" he cried.

"Get up, go into Damascus," was the reply; "and you will be told what to do."

Still groping in darkness, Saul was led by some fellow-travellers into the city. And there a man named Ananias came to him in the Street Called Straight and said, "Brother Saul, the Lord Jesus has sent me, so that you may receive your sight and be filled with the Holy Spirit."

Then Saul's eyes were opened. Among the disciples in Damascus for a number of days he was fed and strengthened, and was baptized a Christian.

At once he began preaching in the synagogues that Jesus was the Son of God.

"But is not this the man who has been killing Christians in Jerusalem, and came here specially to arrest them and take them to the high priests?" they cried in amazement.

But Saul, who was now called Paul, grew stronger and stronger in testifying of Christ.

And the Jews of Damascus banded together to kill him. But their plan was known to the Christians, and during the night they let Paul down over the wall in a basket.

So Paul went back to Jerusalem, and joined the disciples there. Despite the hatred of Jew and Gentile he spread the good tidings far and wide, visiting the Christian churches, encouraging them, and writing letters of counsel and tender rebuke and exhortation.

"Wake up, sleeper!" he called; "Come out from death, and Christ will give you light!"

On a certain evening he was preaching in an upper room. And about midnight one of his listeners, a young man named Eutychus, grew drowsy with the lamplight and the long speech, and fell out of a third story window. When they went to lift him up, the lad was dead.

Paul took him in his arms, saying, "Do not be alarmed, for his life is in him."

And Paul went upstairs again and continued speaking until the light dawned. And the lad was brought alive, to the great joy of all.

So Paul went his way, carrying the good word, the Gospel. And there were in every country some who heard him gladly and accepted the way of Christ, and some who hated and stoned him, until his life was in constant danger.

But, with persecution, the Church grew more and more. Over land and sea the good news swept like flames that cannot be stopped. Though Christians were martyred, given to the lions and tortured at the stake, still they continued to sing and pray, to preach and to heal, taking the Gospel into Asia and Africa and Europe, to the islands of the sea, and to the farthest parts of the world.

Paul has written a message for all time in his Epistle to the Romans:

KING JAMES VERSION

The Spirit itself beareth witness with our spirit, that we are the children of God: and if children, then heirs; heirs of God, and joint-heirs with Christ; if so be that we suffer with him, that we may be also glorified together.

And we know that all things work together for good to them that love God, to them who are the called according to his purpose.

Who shall separate us from the love of Christ? shall tribulation, or distress, or persecution, or famine, or nakedness, or peril, or sword?

Nay, in all these things we are more than conquerors through him that loved us.

For I am persuaded that neither death, nor life, nor angels, nor principalities, nor powers, nor things present, nor things to come, nor height, nor depth, nor any other creature, shall be able to separate us from the love of God, which is in Christ Jesus our Lord.

REFERENCES: KING JAMES VERSION

REFERENCES: KING JAMES VERSION

THE REFERENCES ARE ARRANGED SO THAT
EACH STORY MAY BE READ CONSECUTIVELY

THE OLD TESTAMENT

IN THE BEGINNING (pp. 13–21)
      Genesis 1:1–31 2:1–9, 15–22 3:1–24

NOAH AND THE ARK (pp. 22–24)
      Genesis 5:3, 4 6:1–22 7:7–24 8:1–17 9:1–14

FAITHFUL ABRAHAM (pp. 27–33)
      Joshua 24:2
      Genesis 11:31 12:1–5 13:14–18 15:1–6 17:1, 5 18:1, 10–14 21:1–6
      24:2–67

JACOB AND ESAU (pp. 34–39)
      Genesis 25:20, 24–34 27:1–44 28:10–21 29:1, 13, 17 30:43 31:3, 17–
      41 32:3–30 33:1–18 49:1, 28

JOSEPH AND HIS BROTHERS (pp. 40–55)
      Genesis 37:3–36 39:1–6, 19–22 40:1–23 41:1–5 . 42:1–38 43:1–34
      44:1–34 45:1–28 46:1–7, 29 47:27

MOSES AND THE COMMANDMENTS (pp. 56–94)
      Exodus 1:5–22 2:1–23 3:1–14 4:1–8, 29–31 5:1–23 6:1, 11, 30
      7:1, 2, 10–14 8:1–15 9:13–35 10:7–29 11:4–7 12:1–13,
      29–39 13:18, 21 14:5–28 15:22–27 16:1–35 17:1–3 19:1–20
      20:1–17 24:12, 24 32:1–20, 30, 31 34:1, 28–35 35:4–28 36:1–
      8, 20 37:1–9, 17–26 38:3 39:8–14 40:17–34
      Numbers 11:4, 5 13:1, 2, 17–33 14:2–9, 20–38 20:1–12 21:10, 23, 33
      22:1–18, 41 23:5–23 24:5–8 33:49–52
      Deuteronomy 5:22 8:1–18 9:4 12:3 29:1–5 34:1–12
      Joshua 1:1, 2 3:15–17 6:1–16, 20

THE NEW TESTAMENT

THE LIGHT OF THE WORLD

MARGINAL SKETCHES (Places and Objects)

The author wishes to thank the following museums for permission to sketch objects in their collections.

Harvard University, Semitic Museum, pp. 27, 158. Cairo Museum of Antiquities, pp. 42, 80. University of Chicago, Oriental Institute, pp. 27, 142, ·168, 174. The British Museum, p. 59

REFERENCE BOOKS

Bagster, Sam'l, & Sons, Ltd.; The Englishman's Greek New Testament, Third Edition. London.

Ballantine, Wm. G., tr.; The Riverside New Testament. Cambridge, Mass. 1923.

Berry, George Ricker; The Interlinear Literal Translation of the Greek New Testament. Chicago, 1897.

Bible, American Revised, New York, 1901.

Bible, Authorized American Corrected. New York, 1911.

La Sainte Bible, Version Synodale. Paris, 1937.

Dakes, John A.; Christ Jesus: The Four Gospels; tr. from the original Greek. Chicago, 1940.

Fenton, Ferrar; The Holy Bible in Modern English. London. Second Edition.

Koldewey, Robert; The Excavations at Babylon. London, 1914.

Lamsa, George M.; The Gospels According to the Eastern Version; tr. from the Aramaic. Philadelphia, 1934.

Martin, G. Currie & Robinson, T. H., editors; Books of the Old Testament in Colloquial Speech. London, 1928–34.

Moffatt, James; The Bible, a New Translation. London, 1935.

The New Testament in Basic English. New York, 1941.

Olmstead, A. T.; History of Assyria. New York, 1923.

Perrot, Georges, & Chipiez, Charles; A History of Art in Chaldea and Assyria; tr. by Armstrong, Walter. London, 1884; New York.

Smith, J. M. Powys & Goodspeed, Edgar; The Bible, an American Translation. Chicago, 1931.

Torrey, Charles Cutler; The Four Gospels. London, 1933. Our Translated Gospels. London, 1936.

The Twentieth Century New Testament, Revised Edition. London, 1904.

Weymouth, Richard Francis; The New Testament in Modern Speech; revised by Robertson, James Alexander; 5th Edition. London, 1937.

Wilson, Sir Charles W.; Jerusalem the Holy City. London, 1889.

Woolley, Sir Leonard; Antiquities of Ur. London, 1929. Abraham. New York, 1936.

8537